This coloring book is for adults, teenagers and children, embark on this adventure and let your creative side emerge

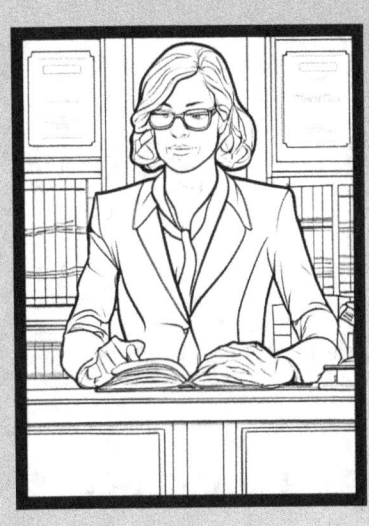

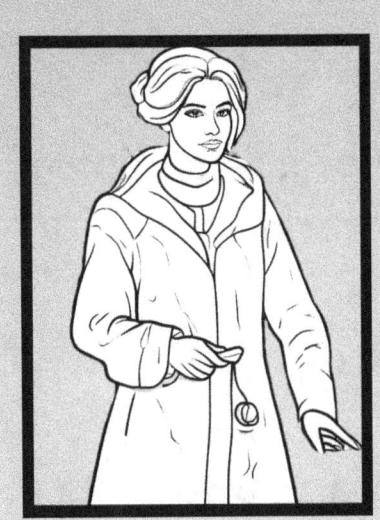

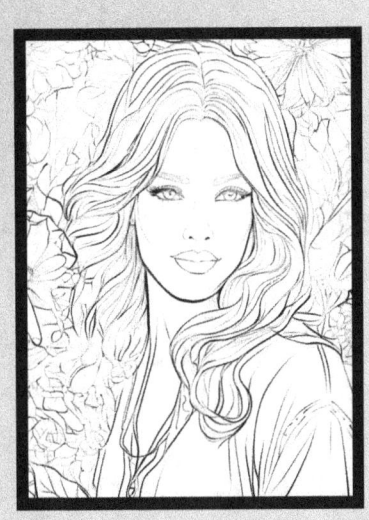

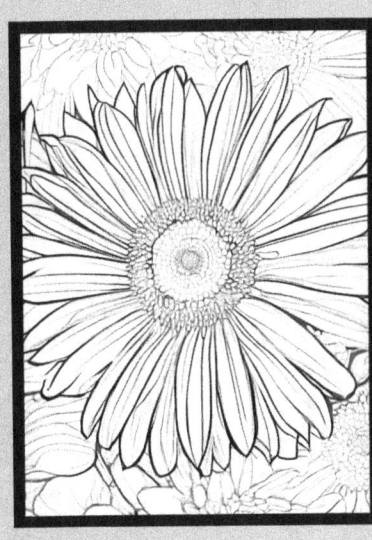

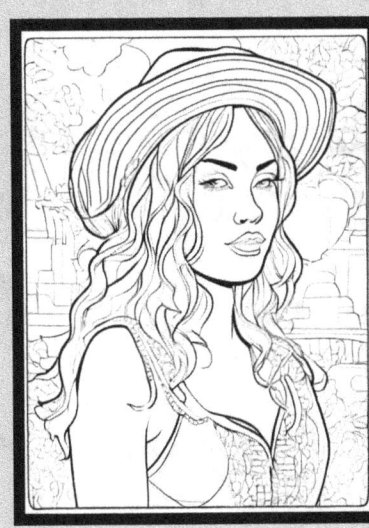

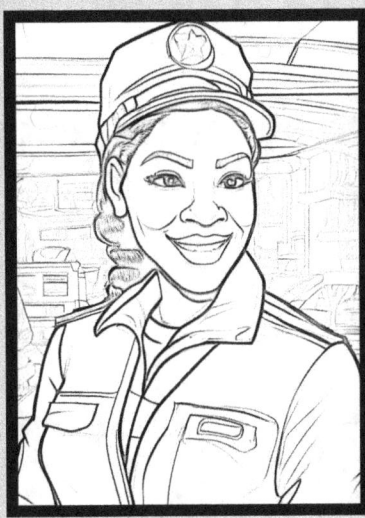

I dedicate this special moment to:

You women whose strength, grace, and resilience light up the pages of this coloring book.

May every stroke of color be a reflection of the unique shine that each of you brings to the world.

May this book be a tribute to your beauty, creativity and power.

May you find joy, serenity and peace when coloring these pages.

reminder that they are truly extraordinary.

With all my respect and admiration, [j.A.F].

....

Test the colors here

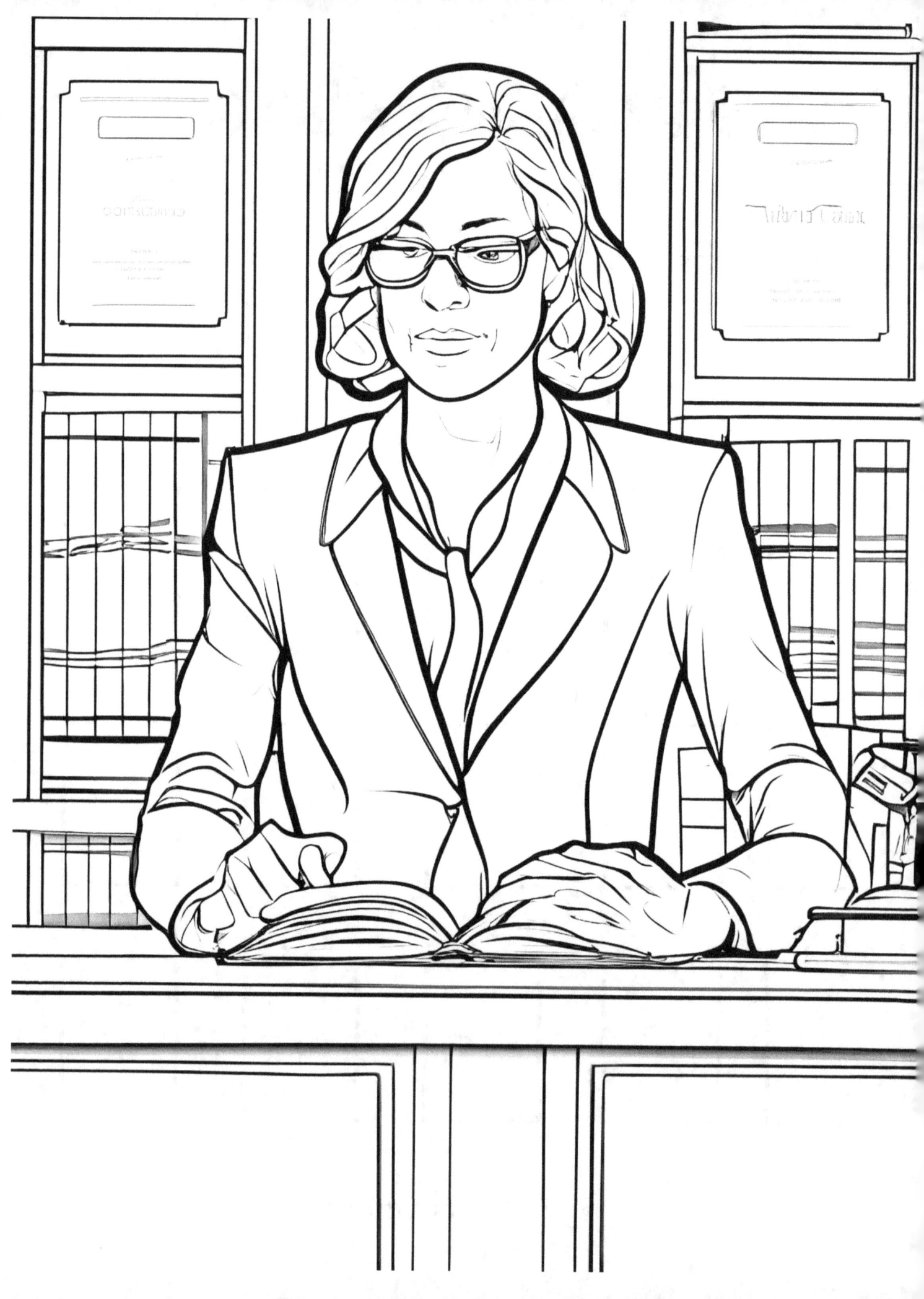

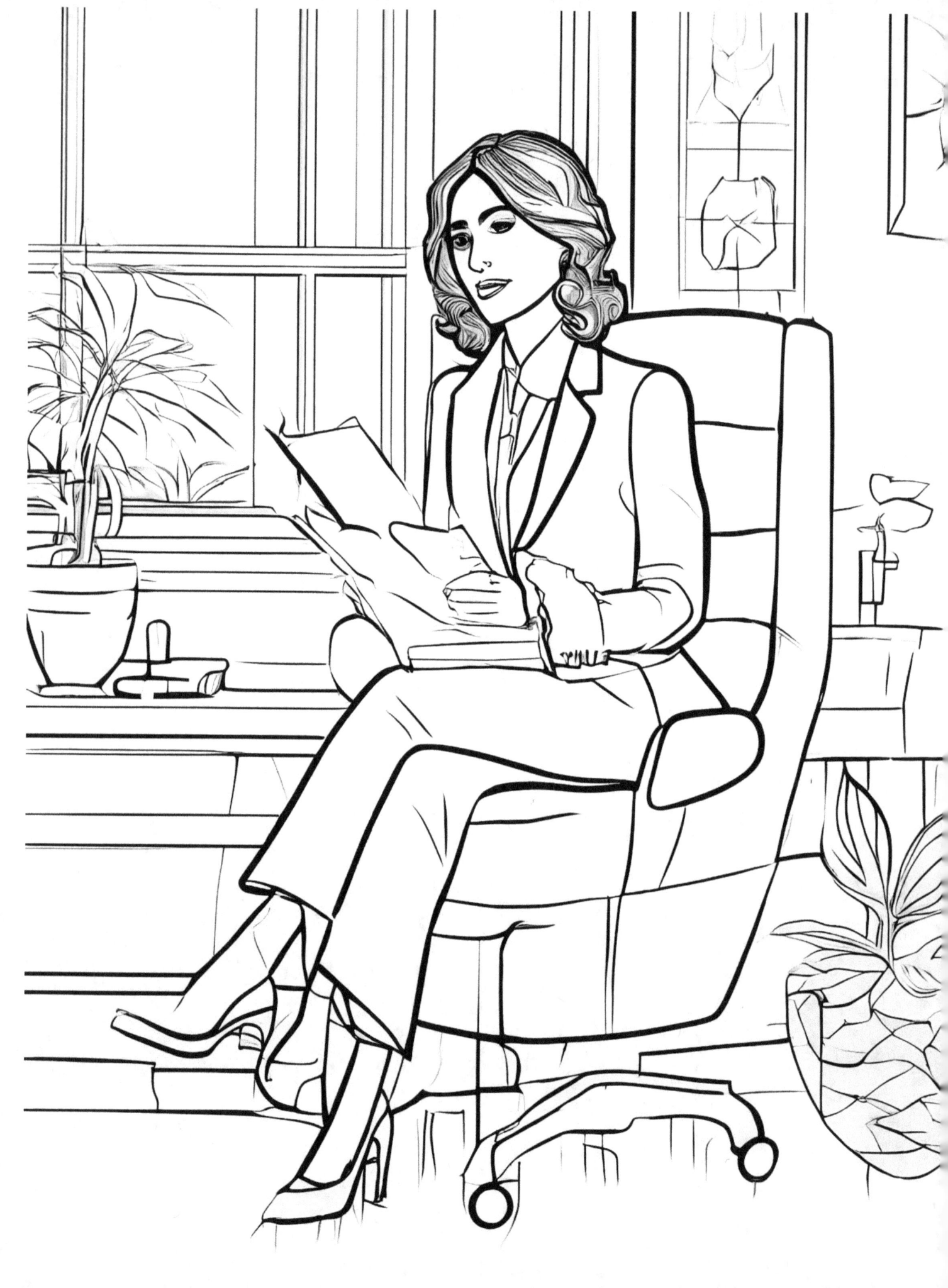

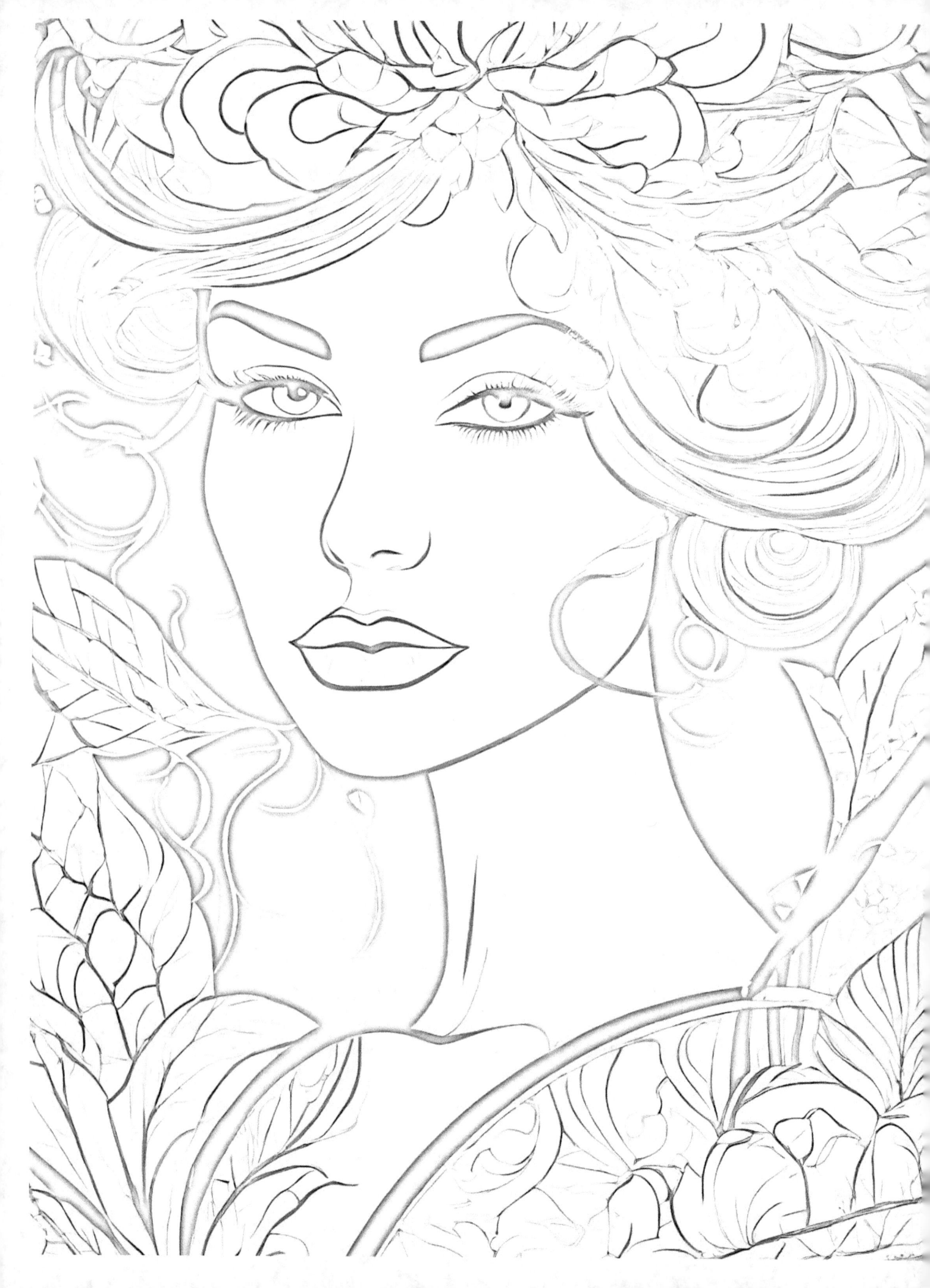

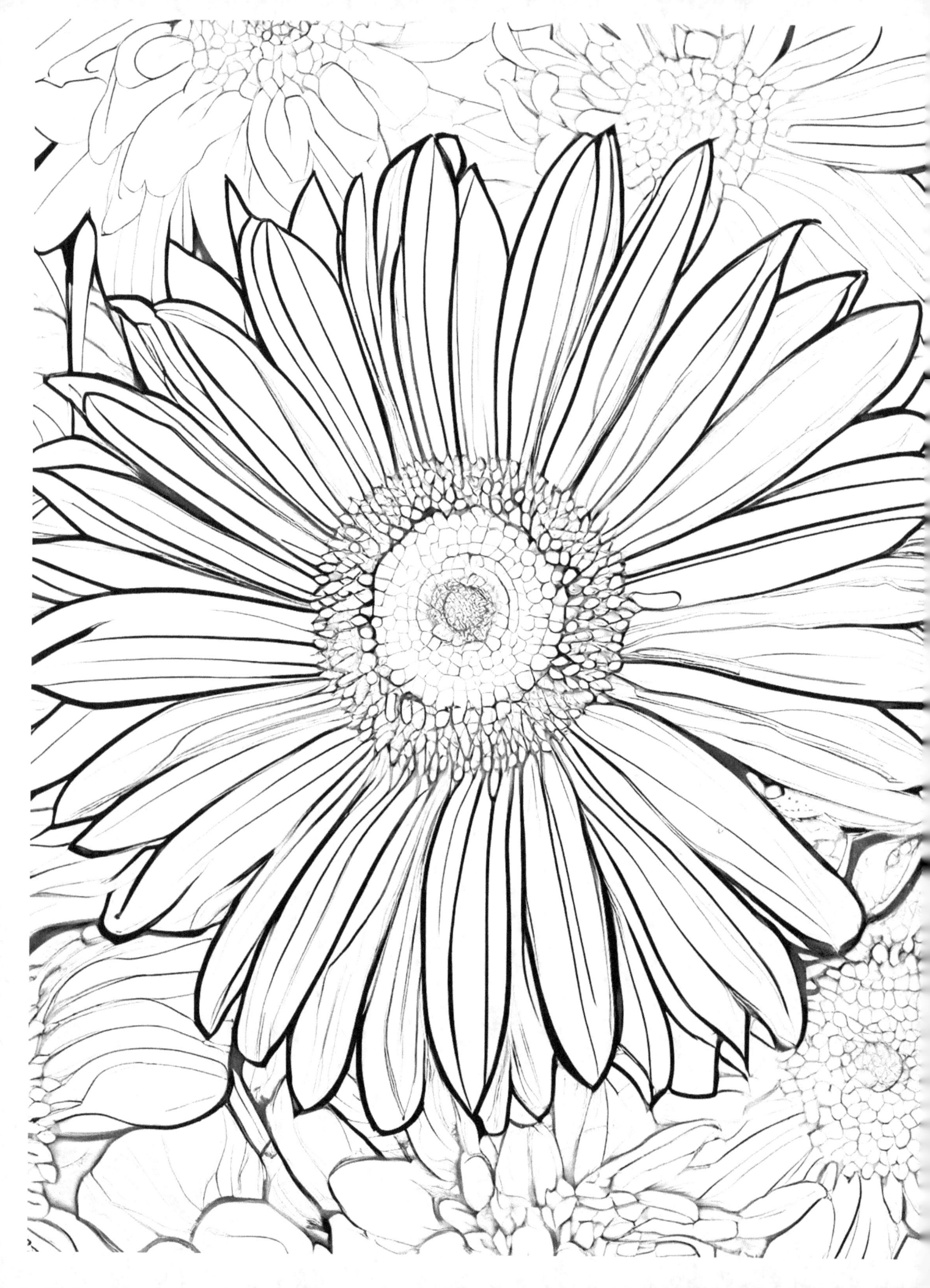

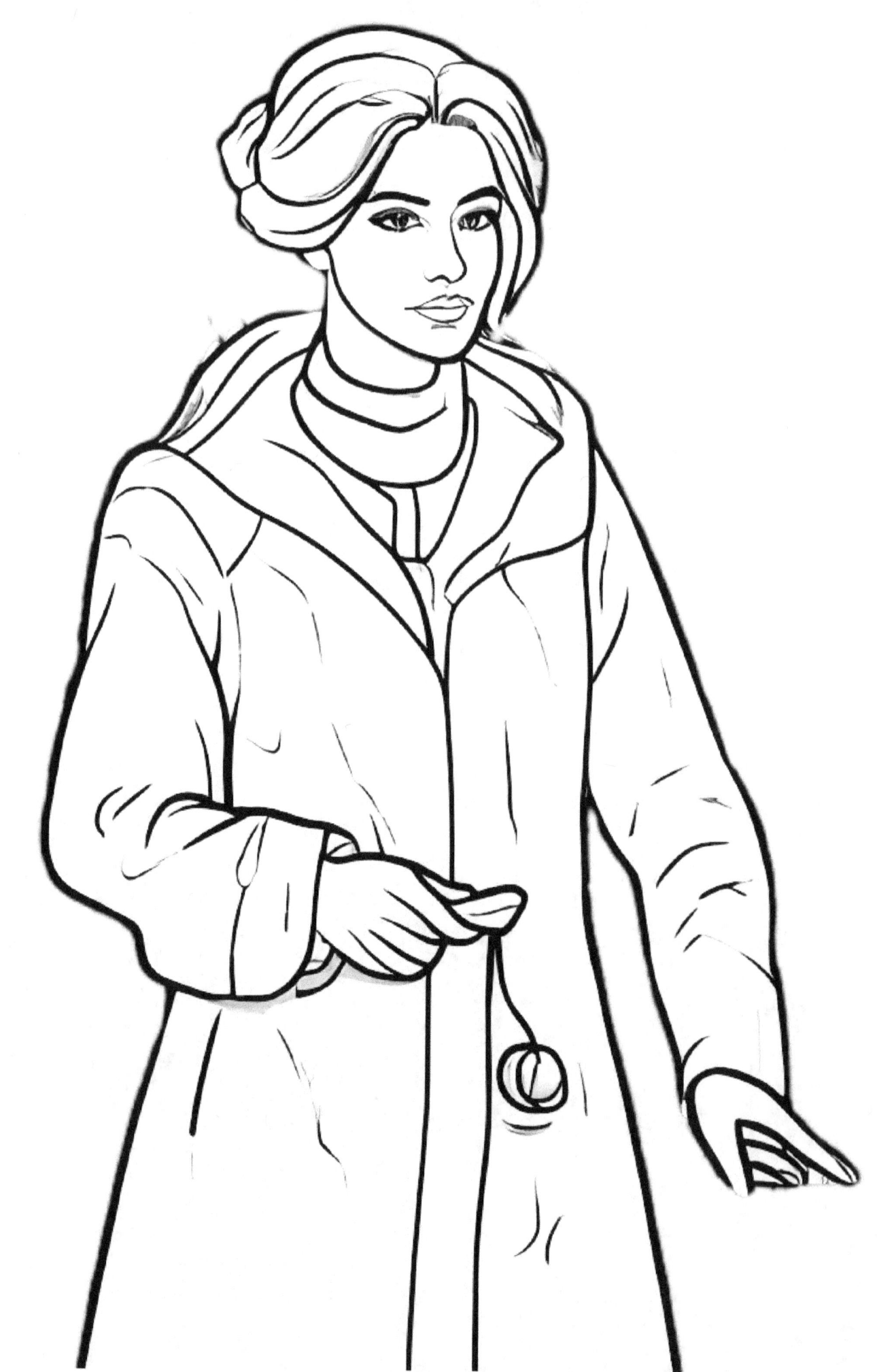

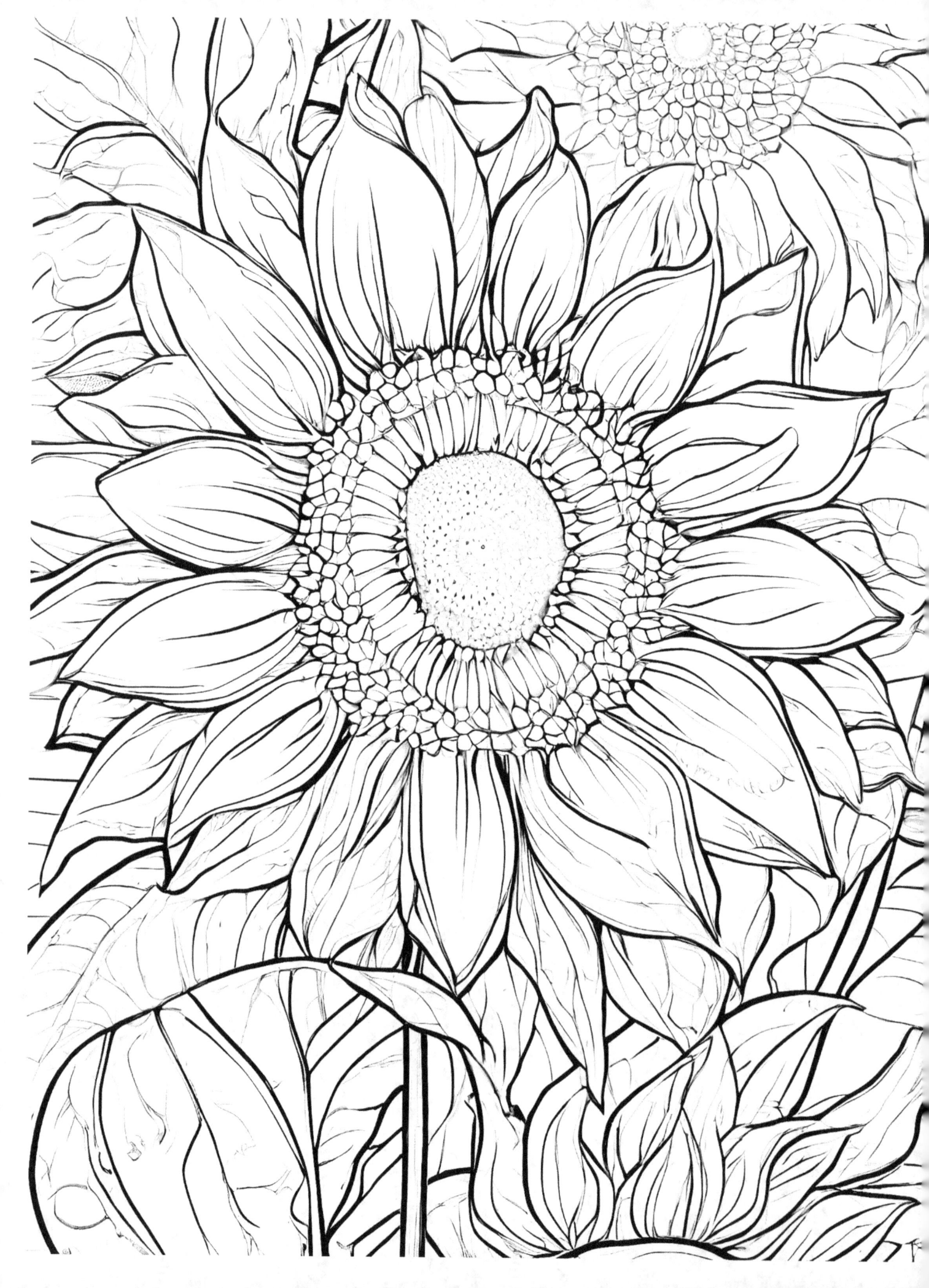

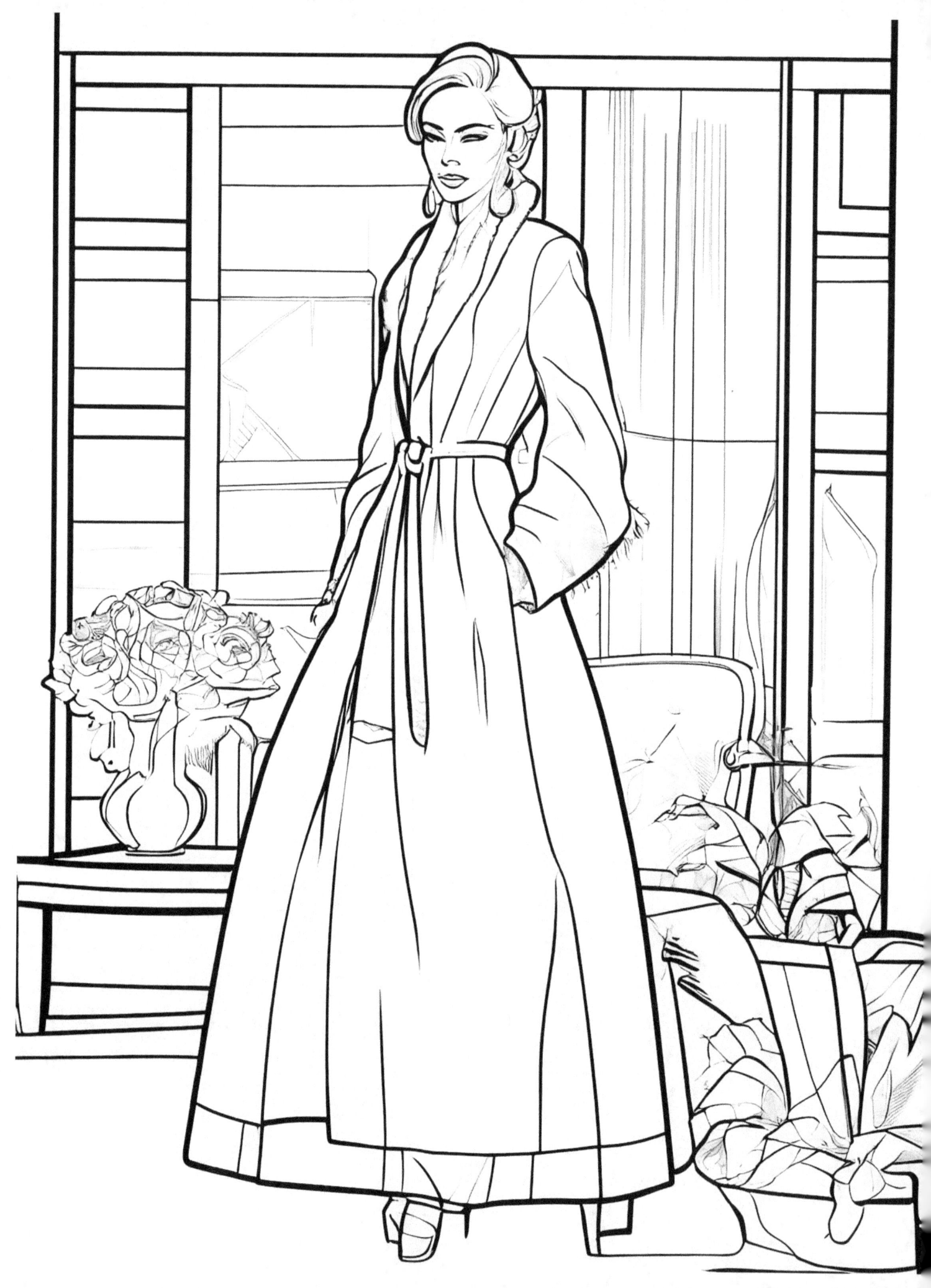

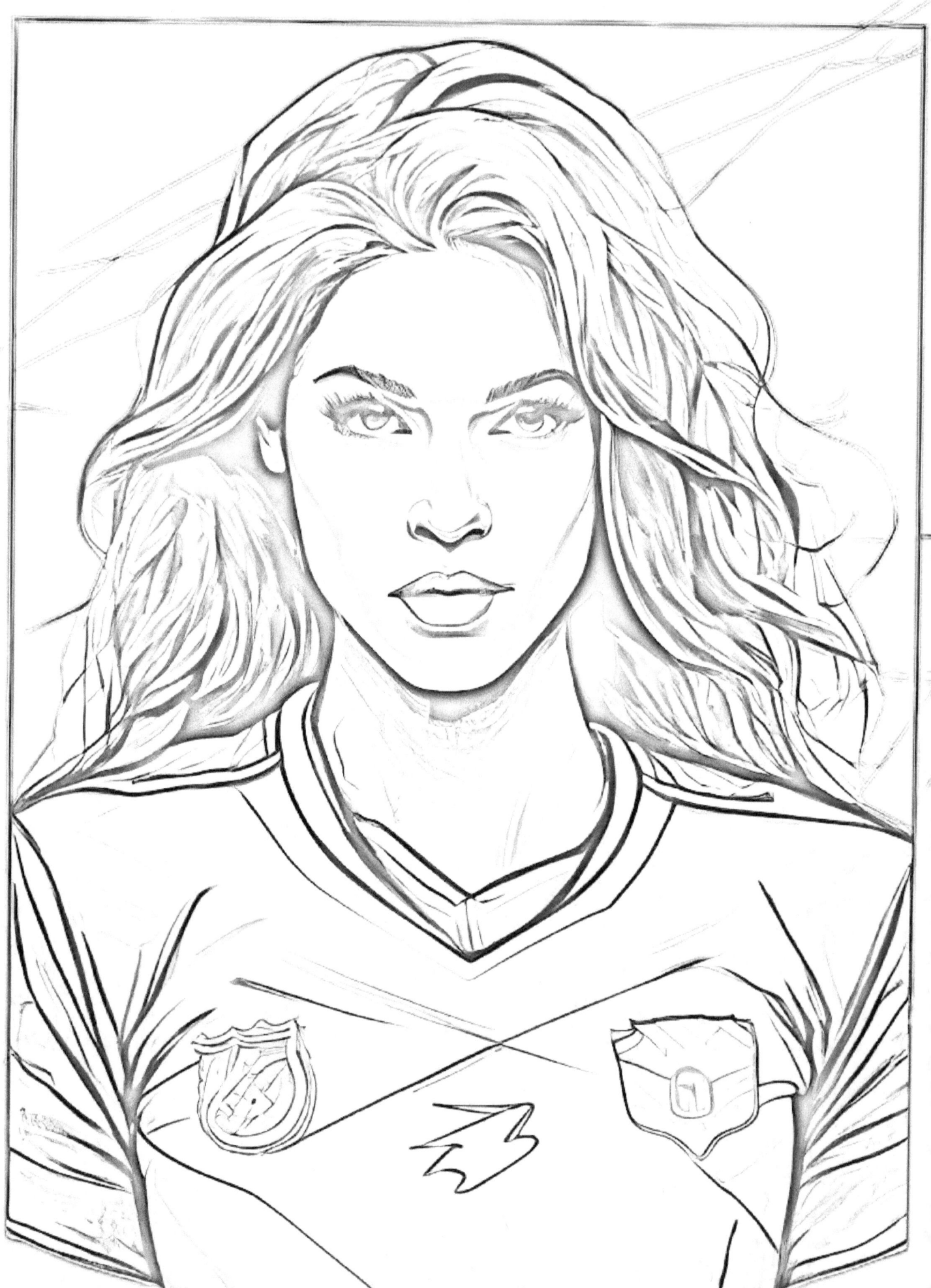

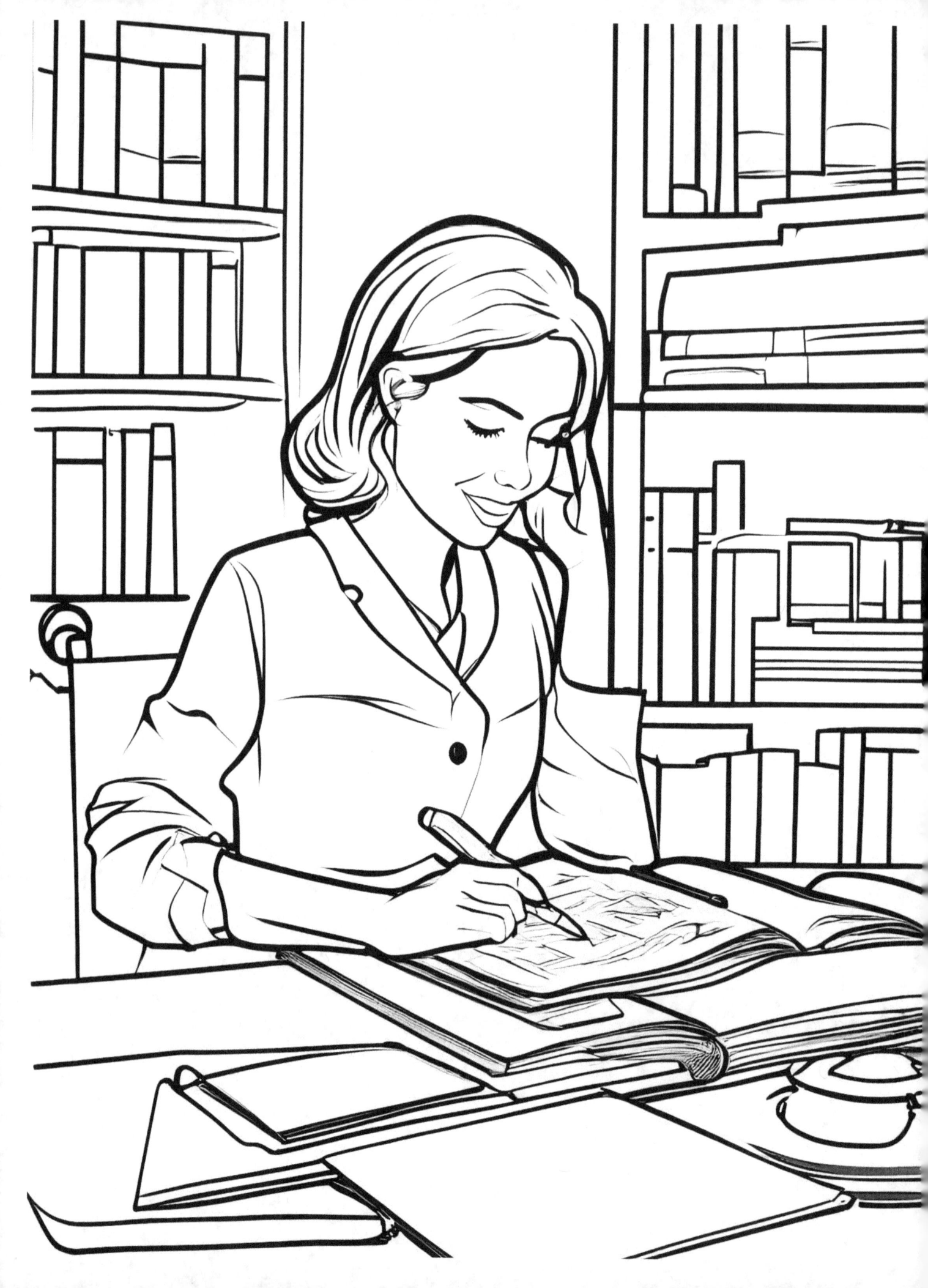

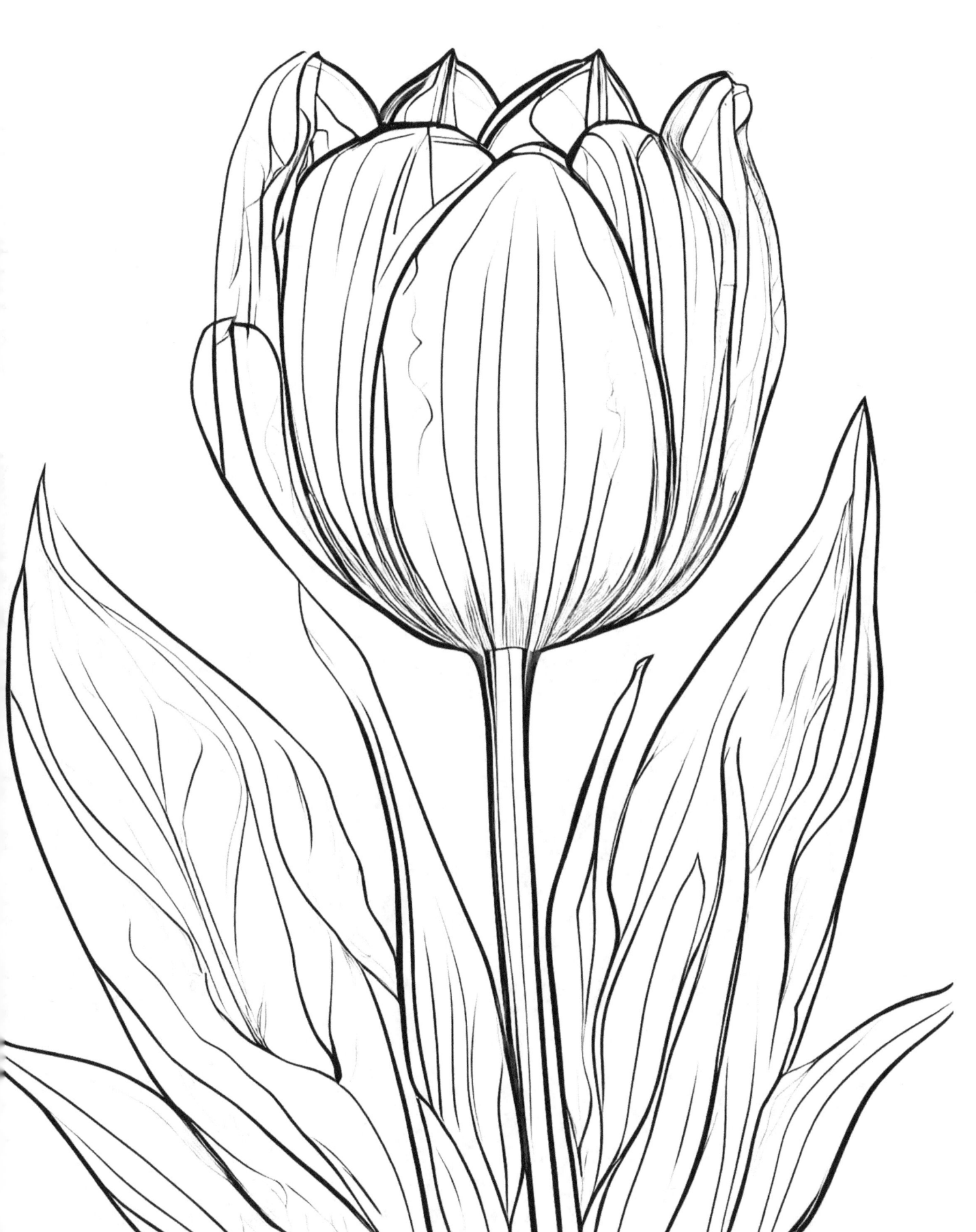

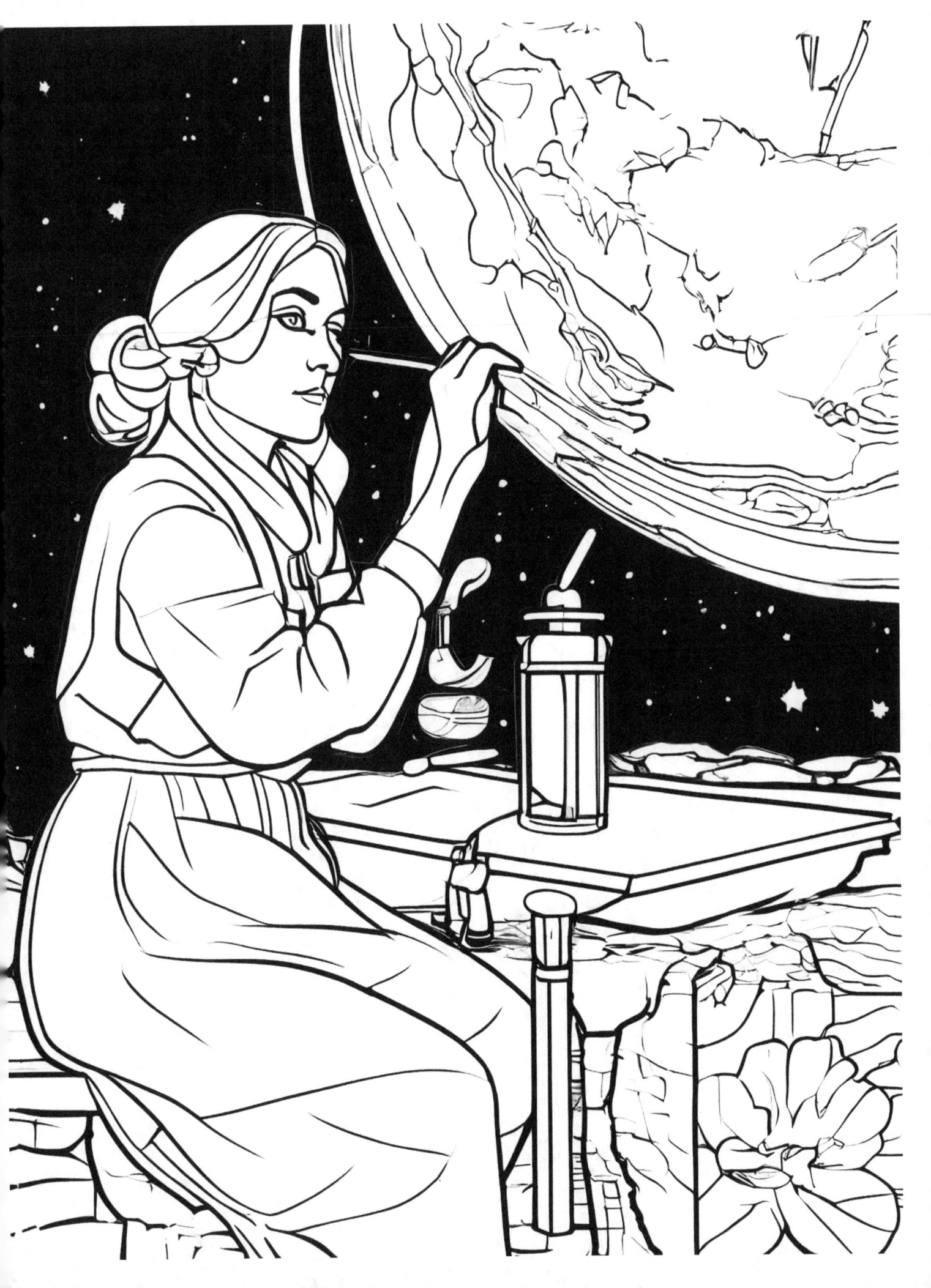

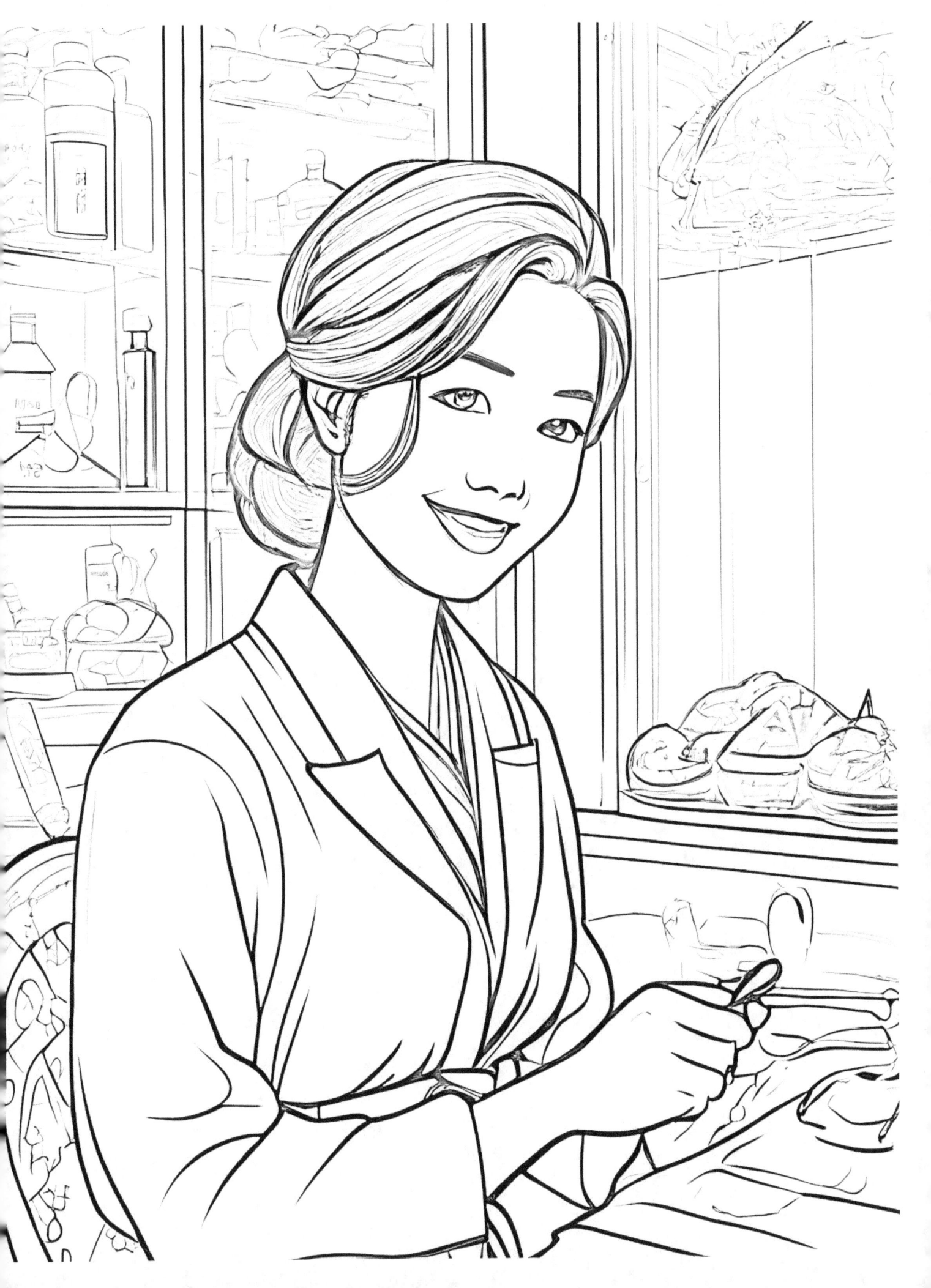

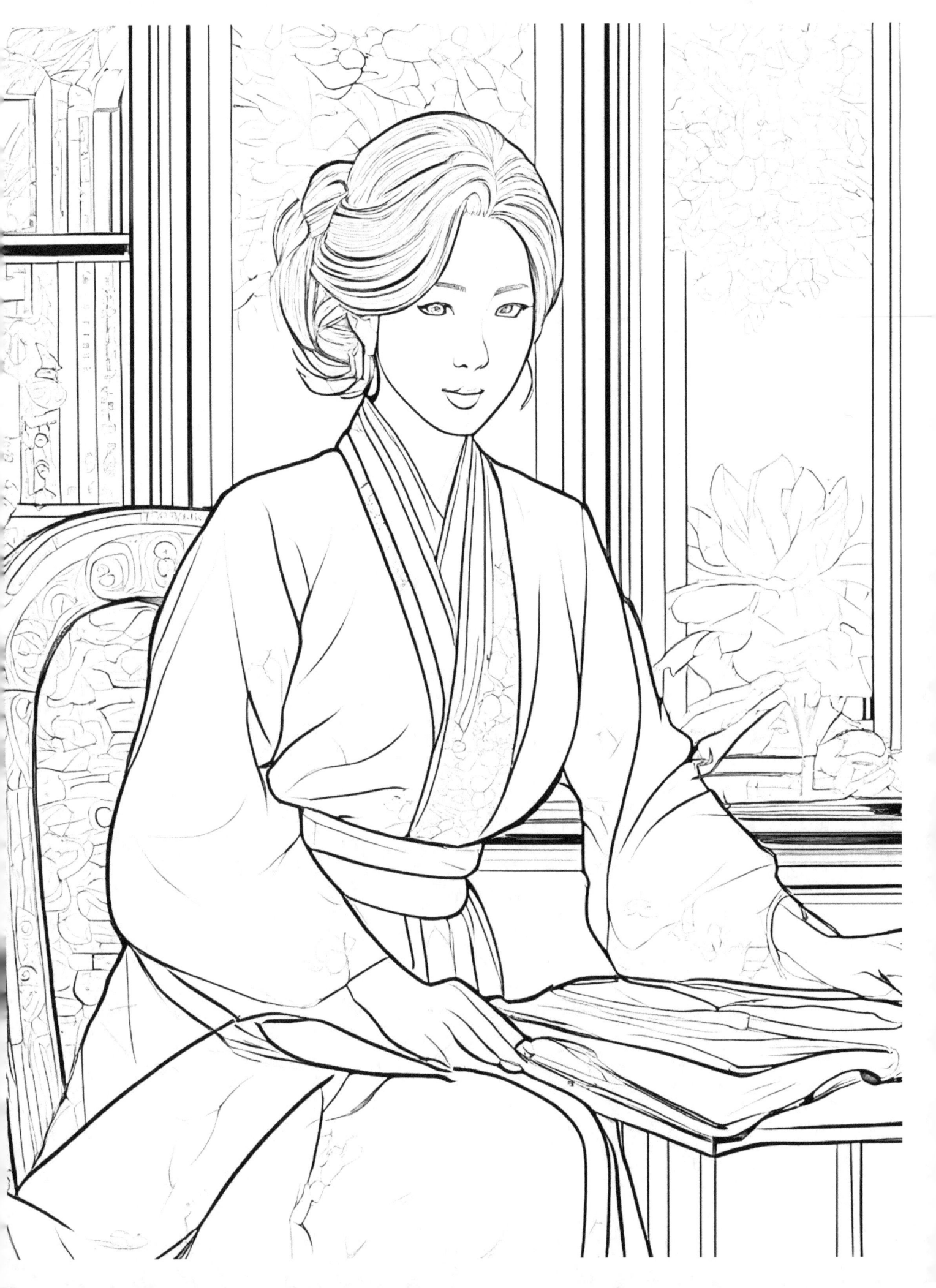

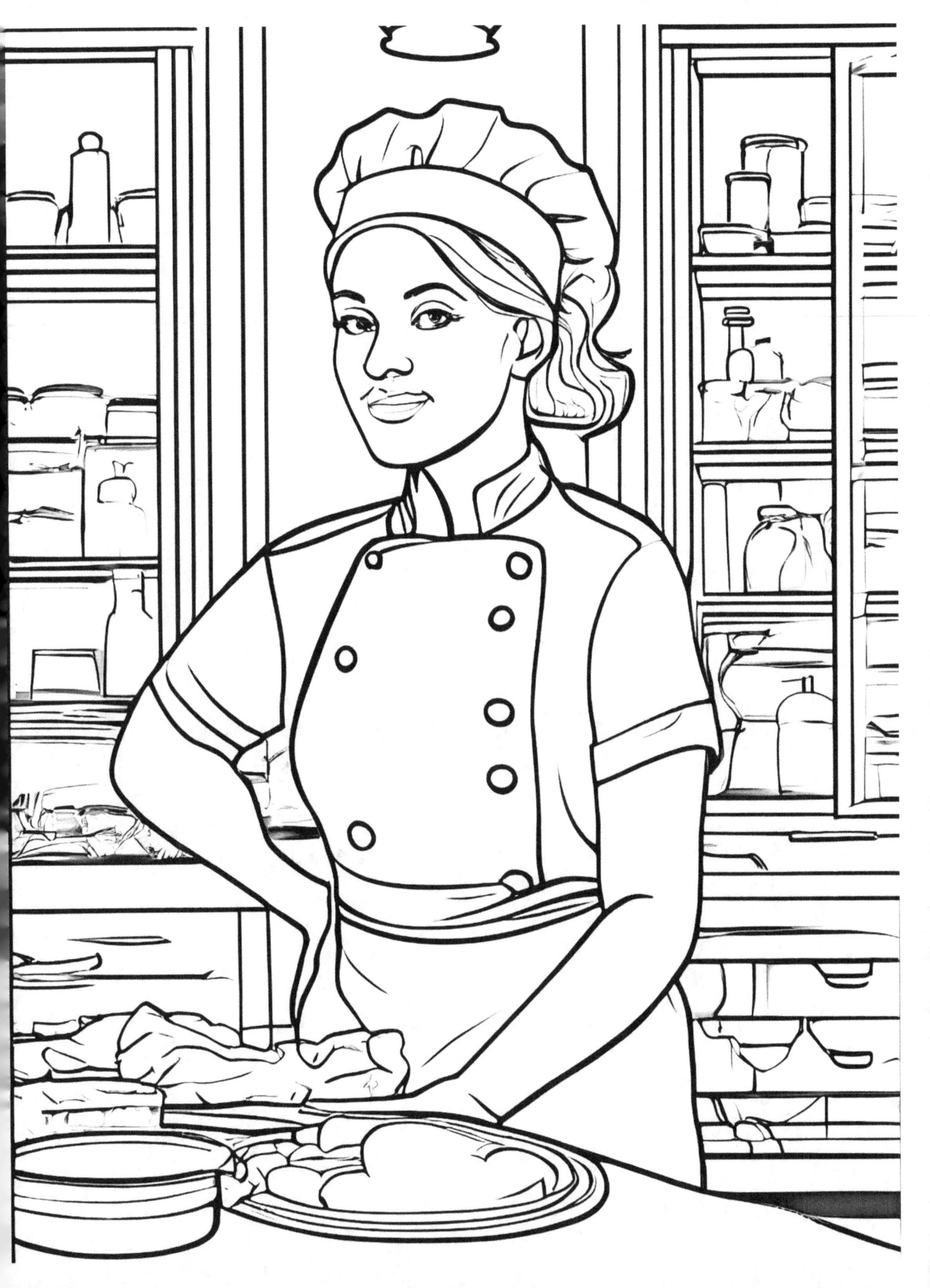

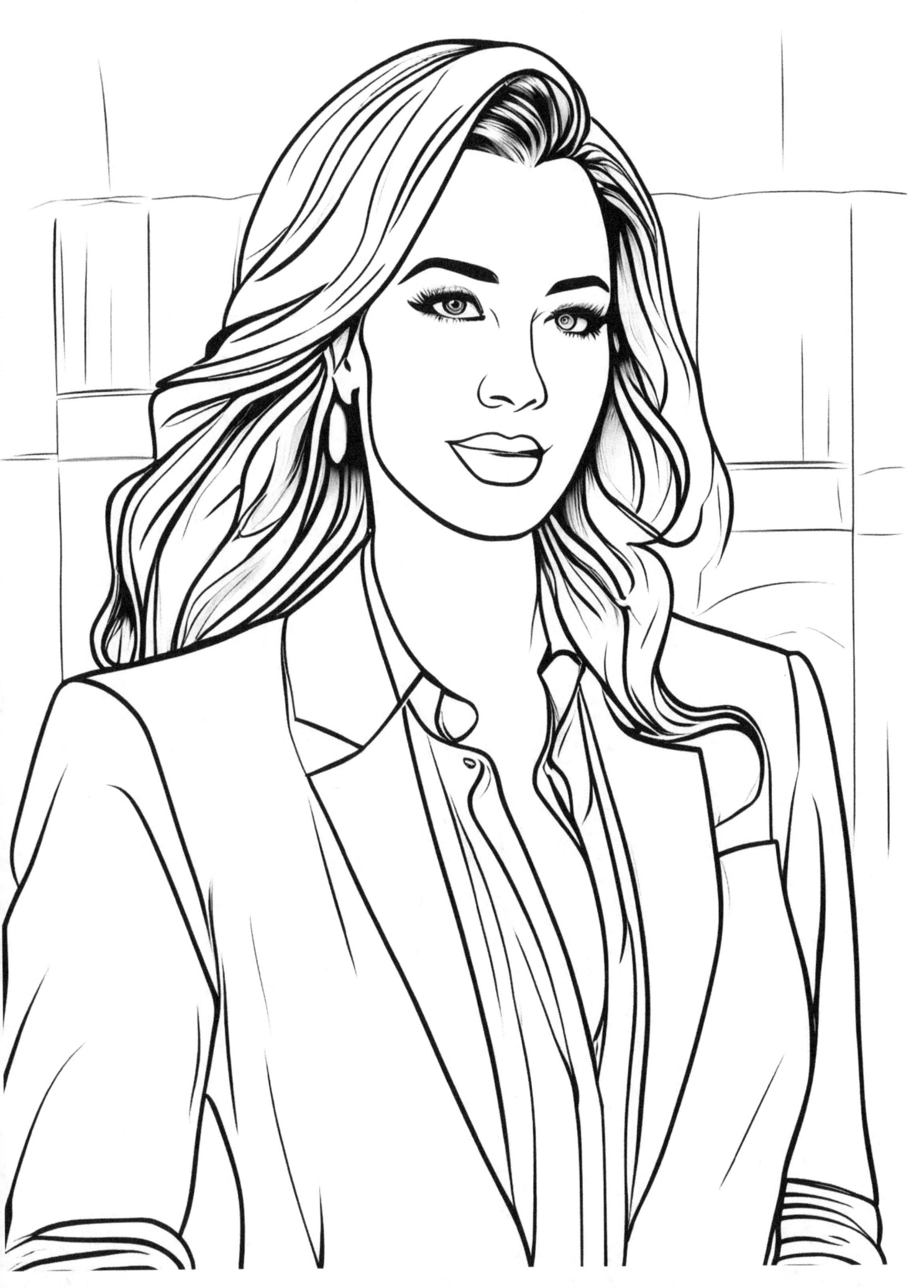

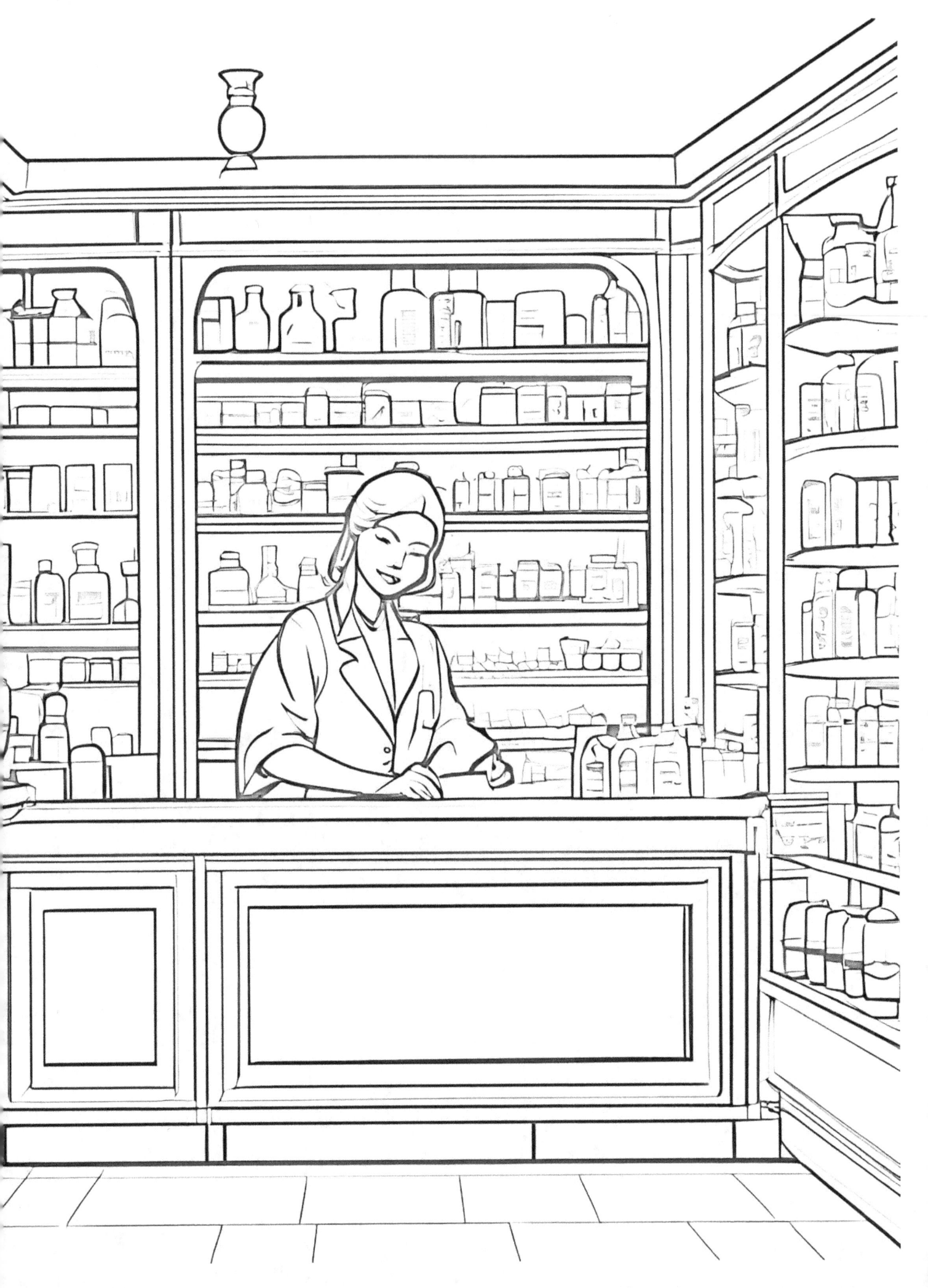

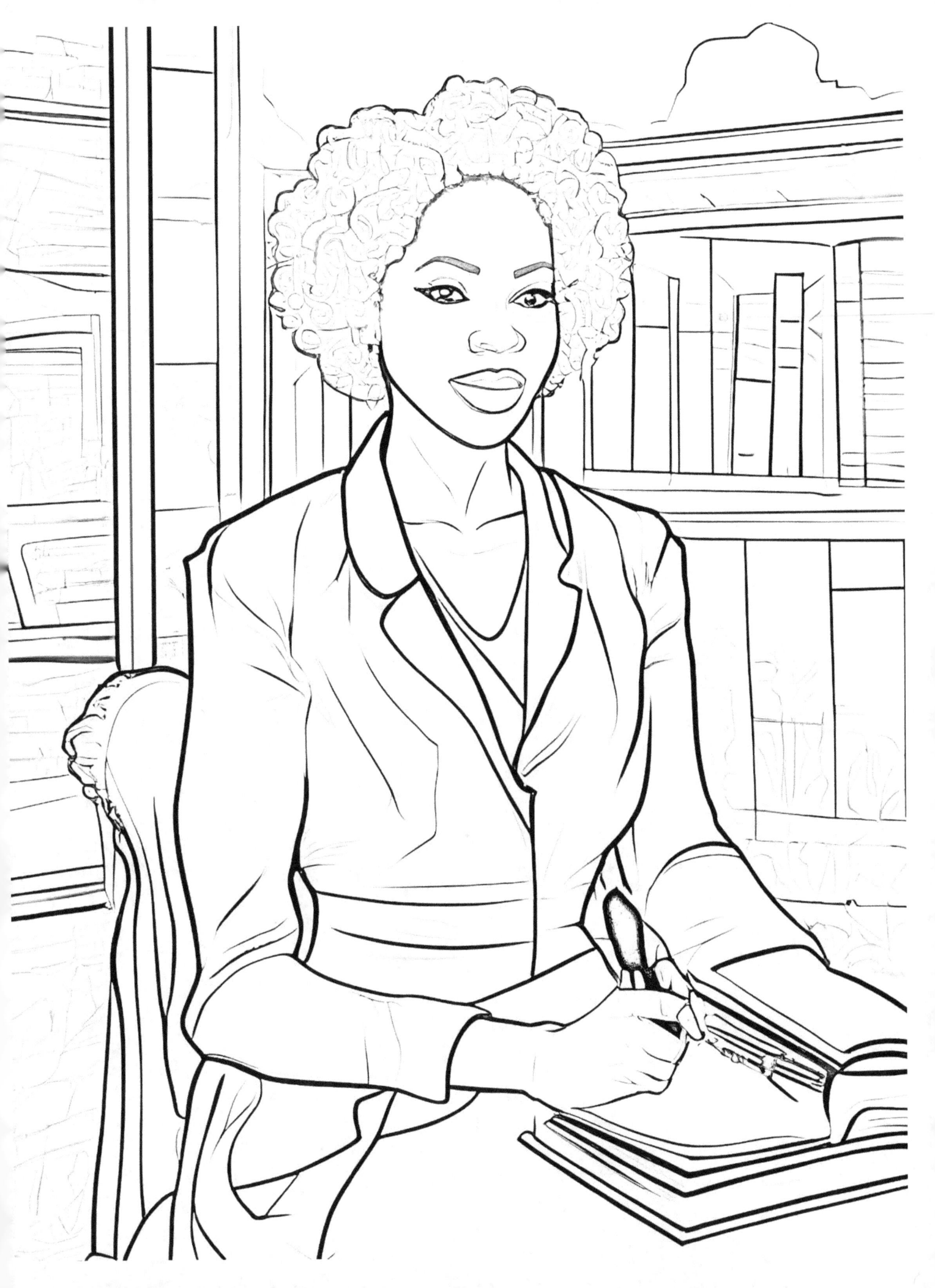

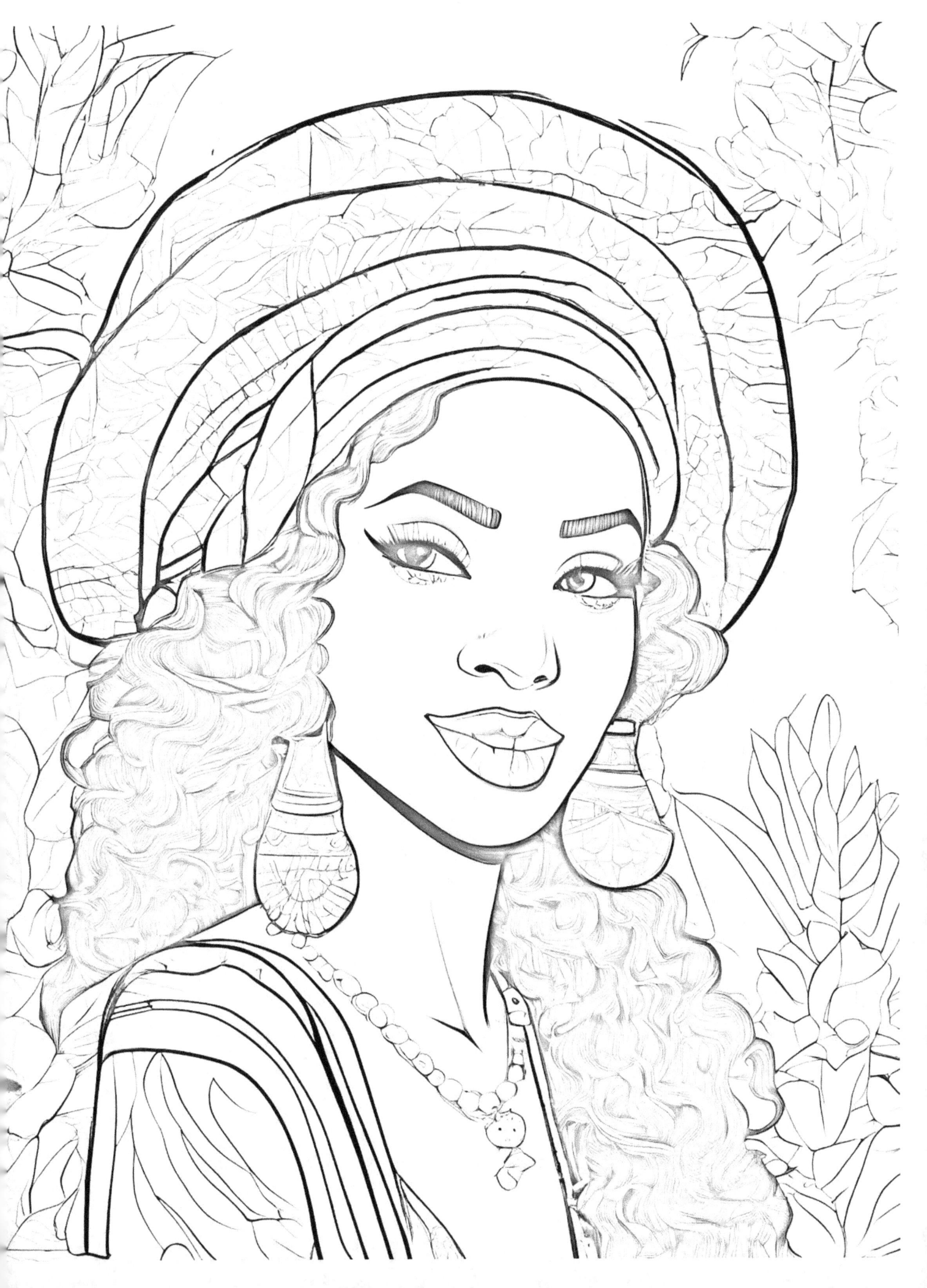

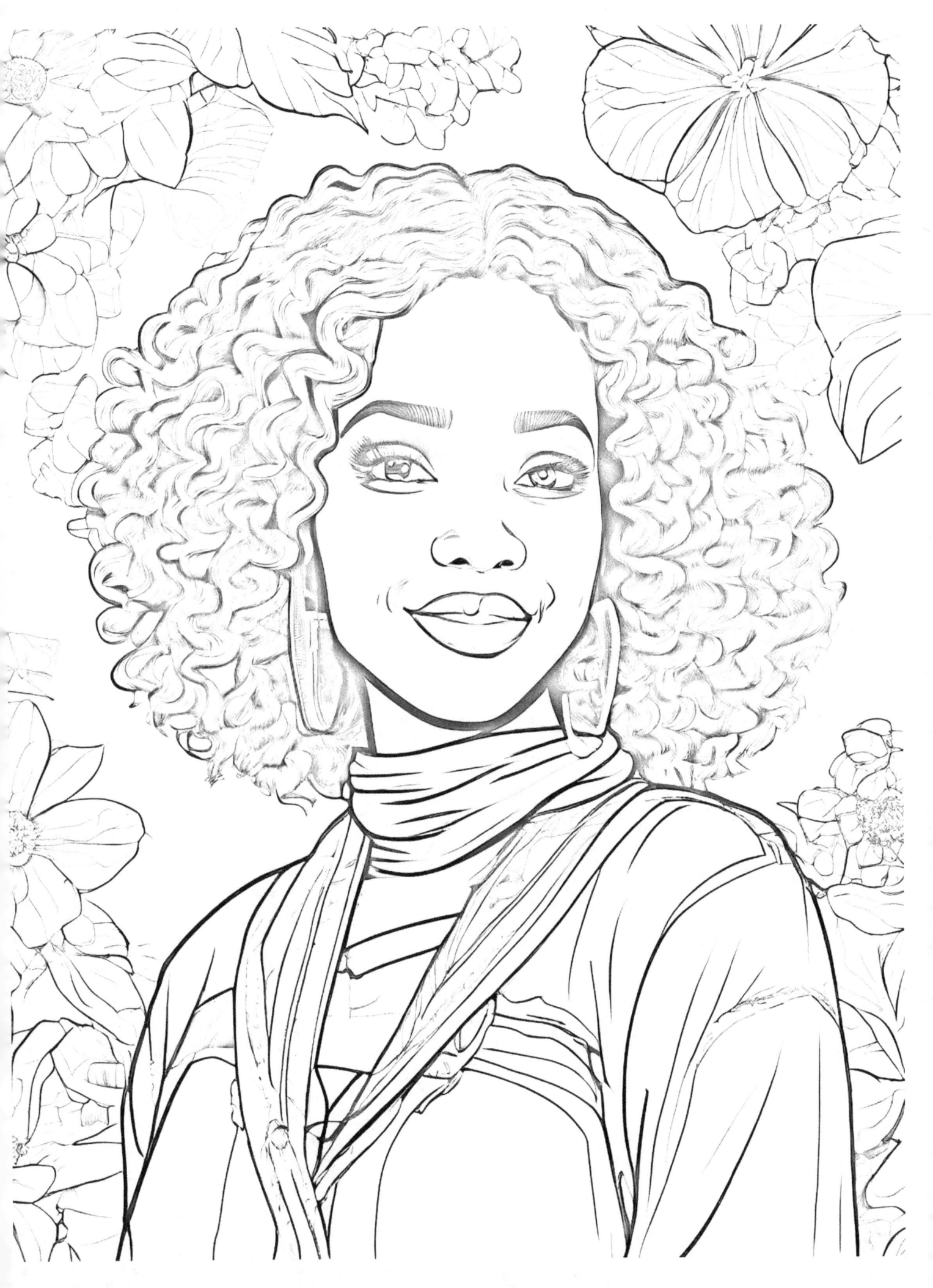

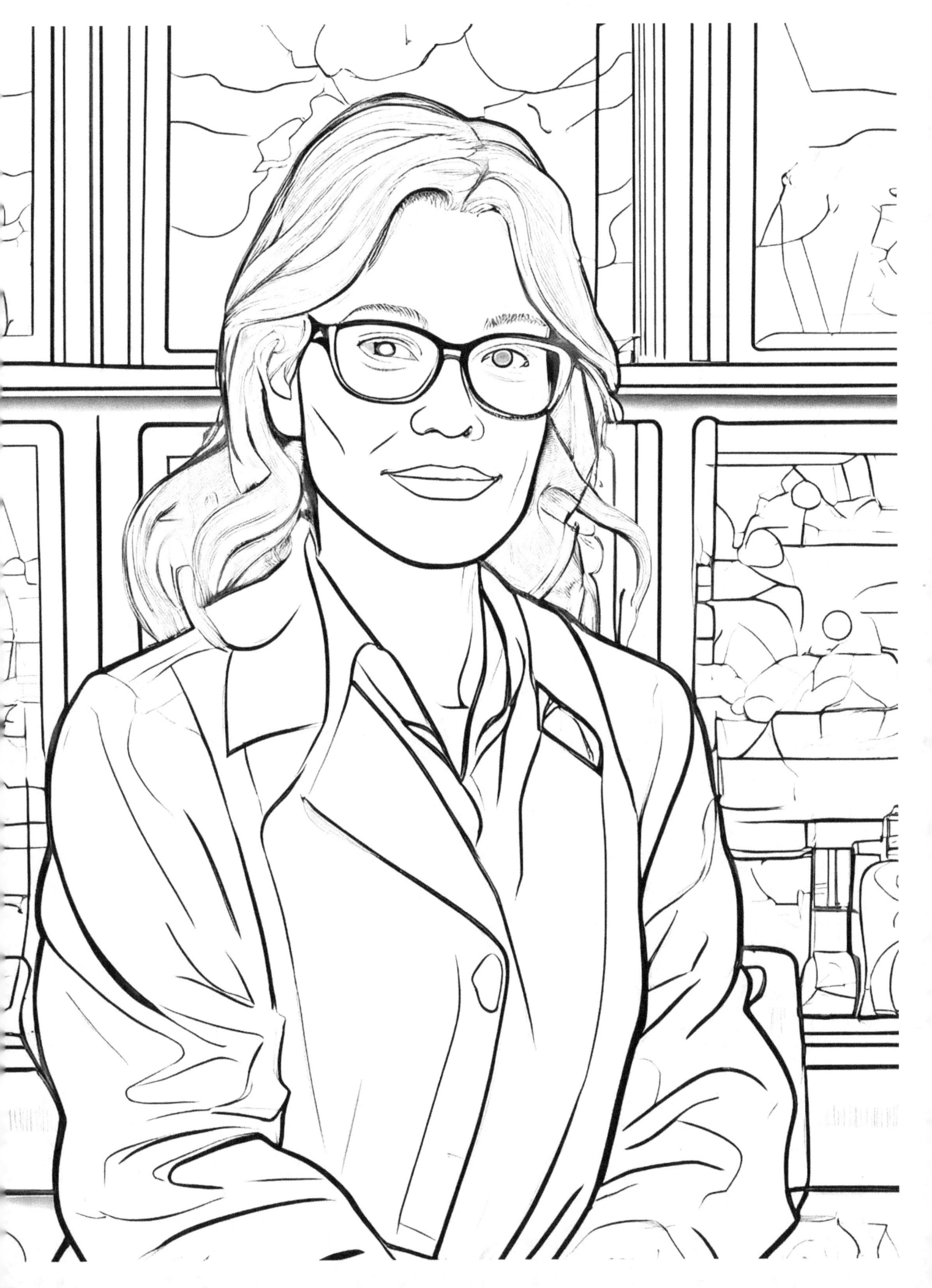

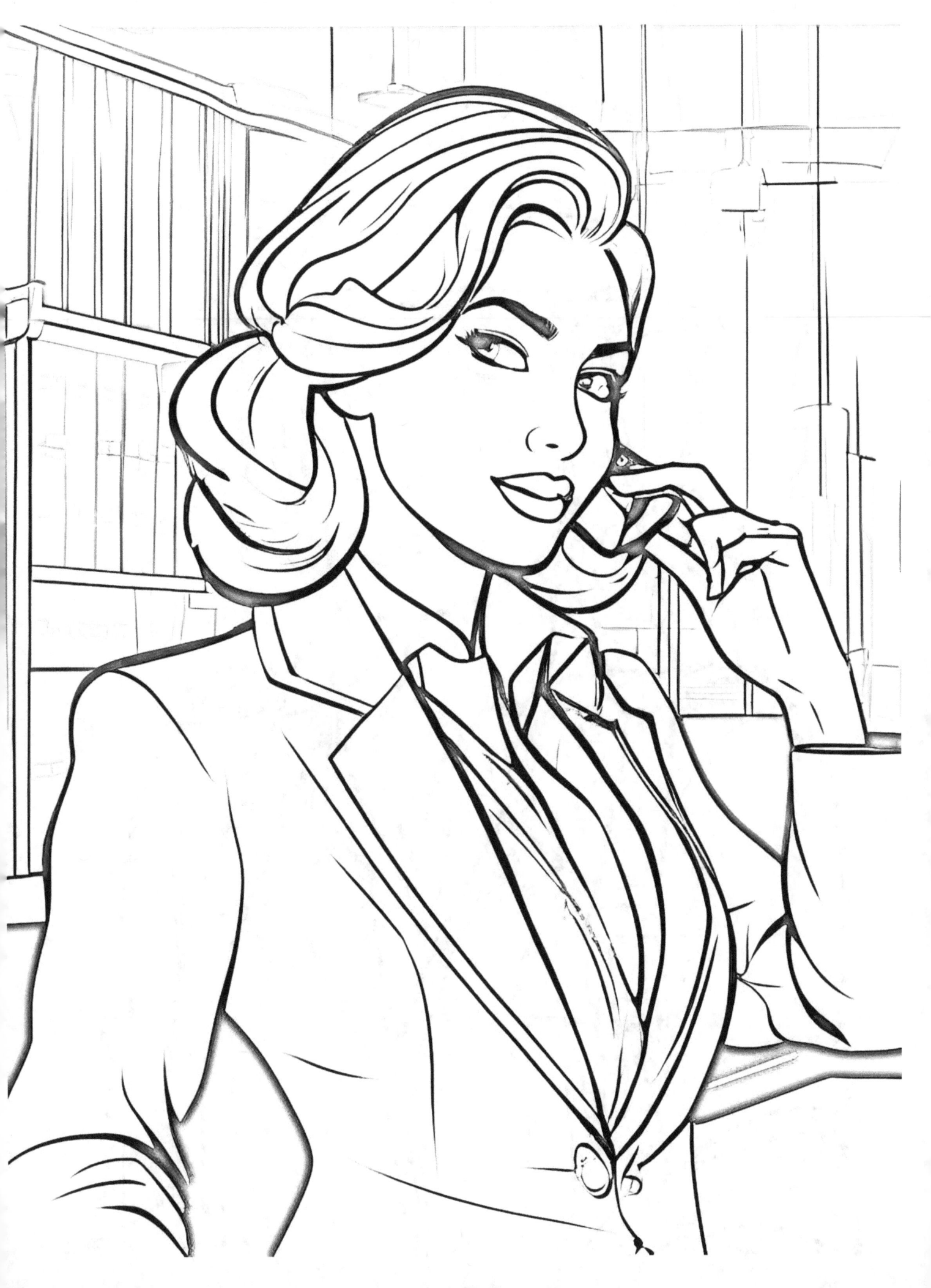

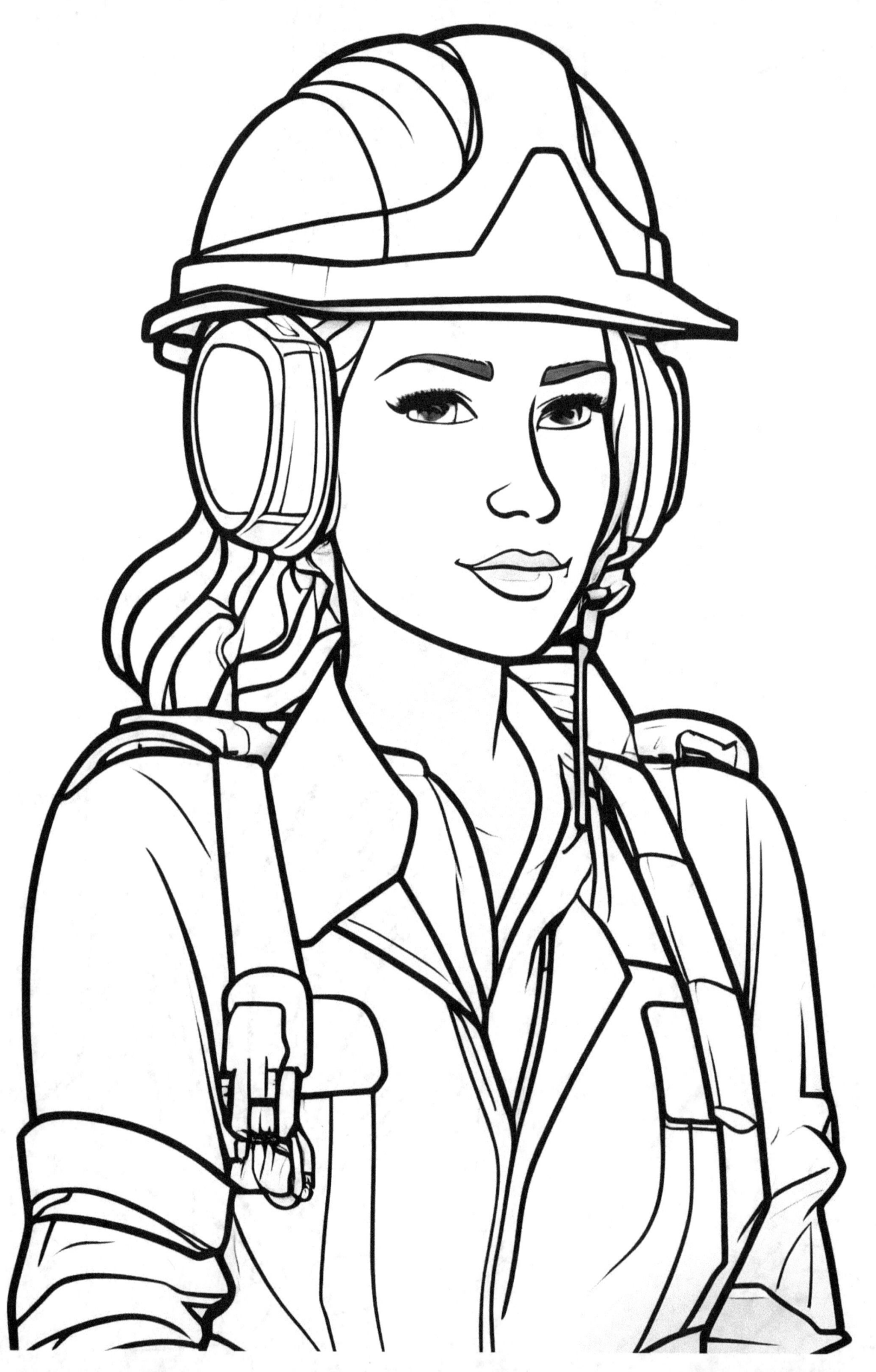

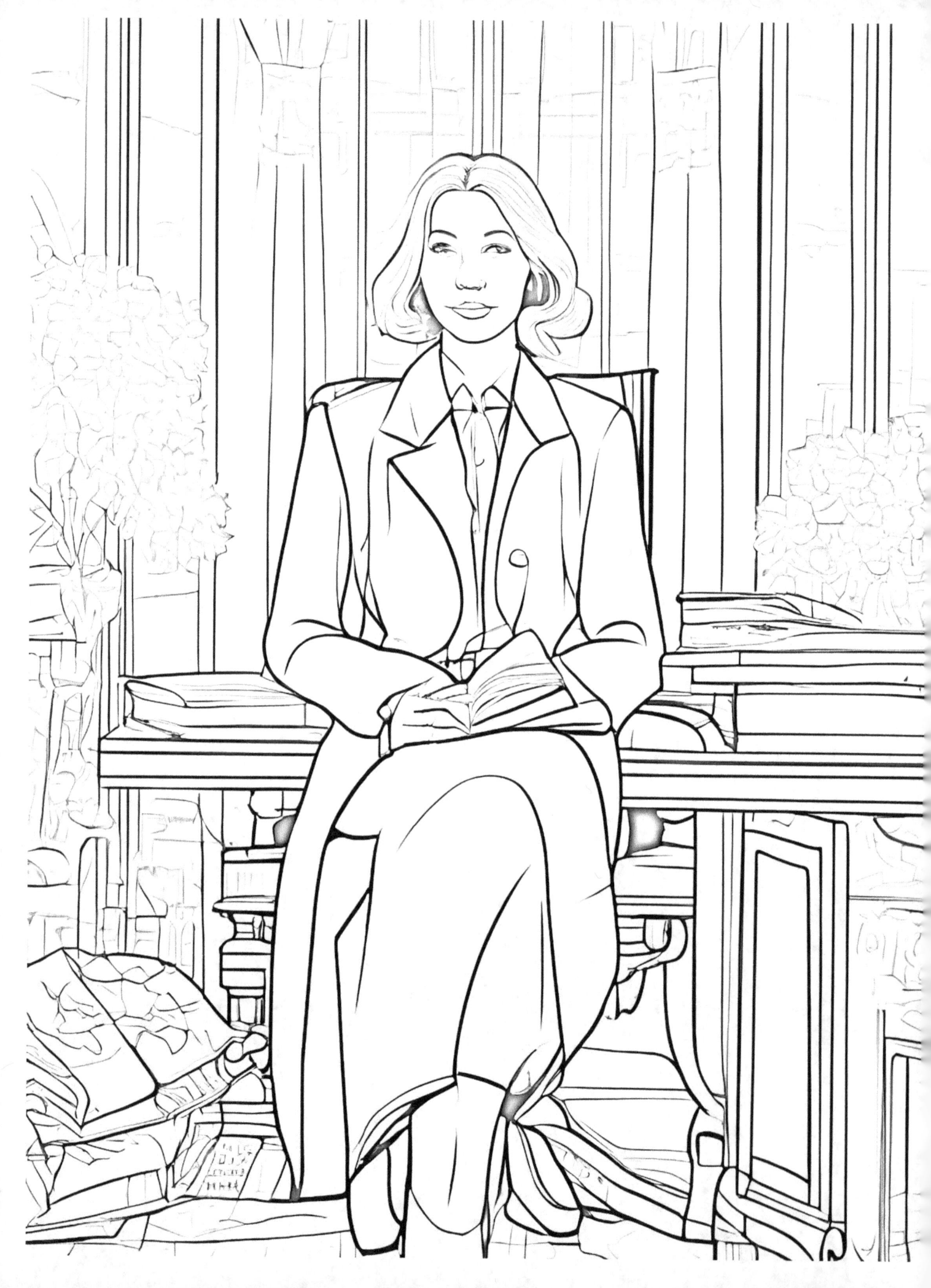

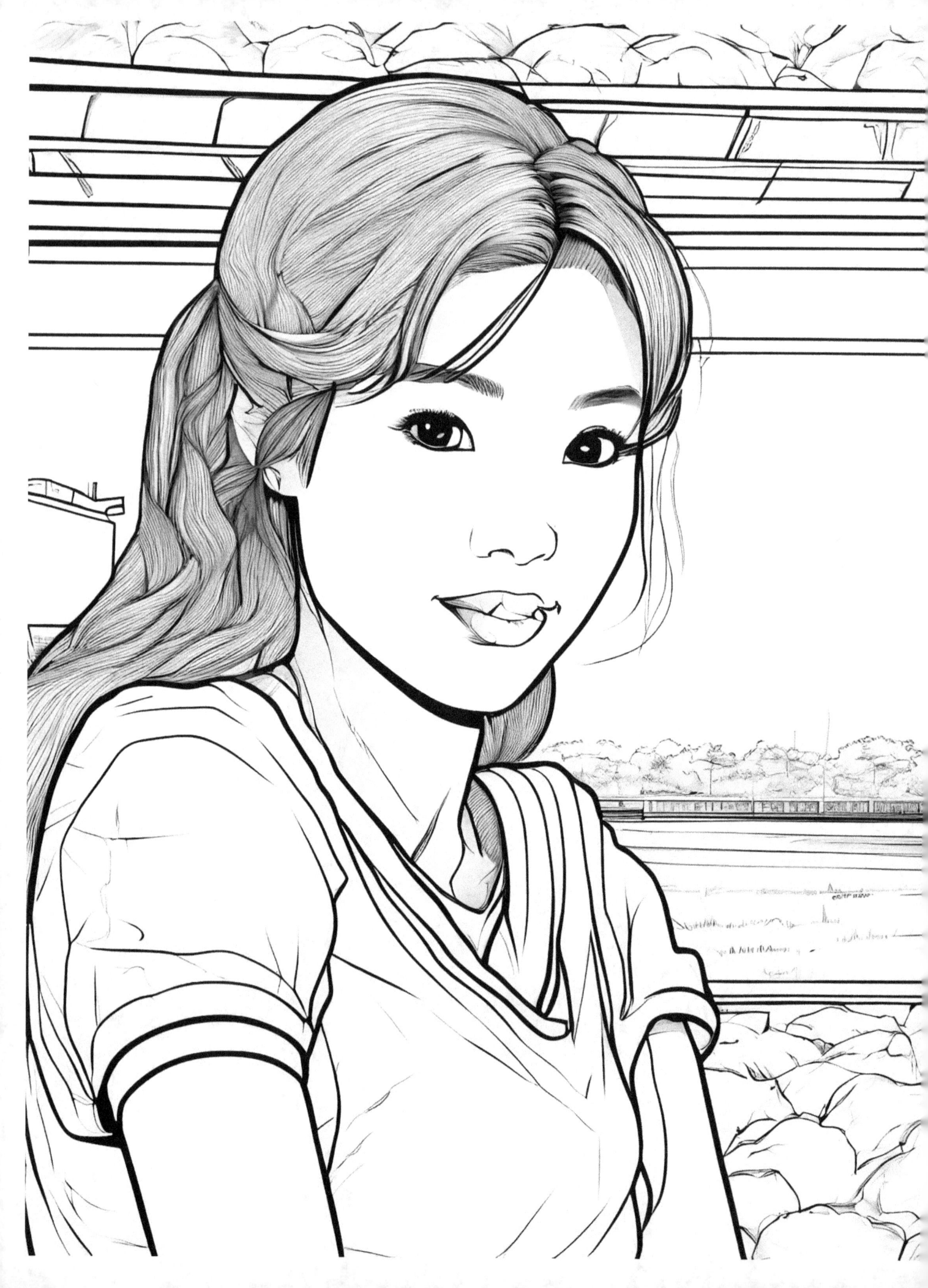

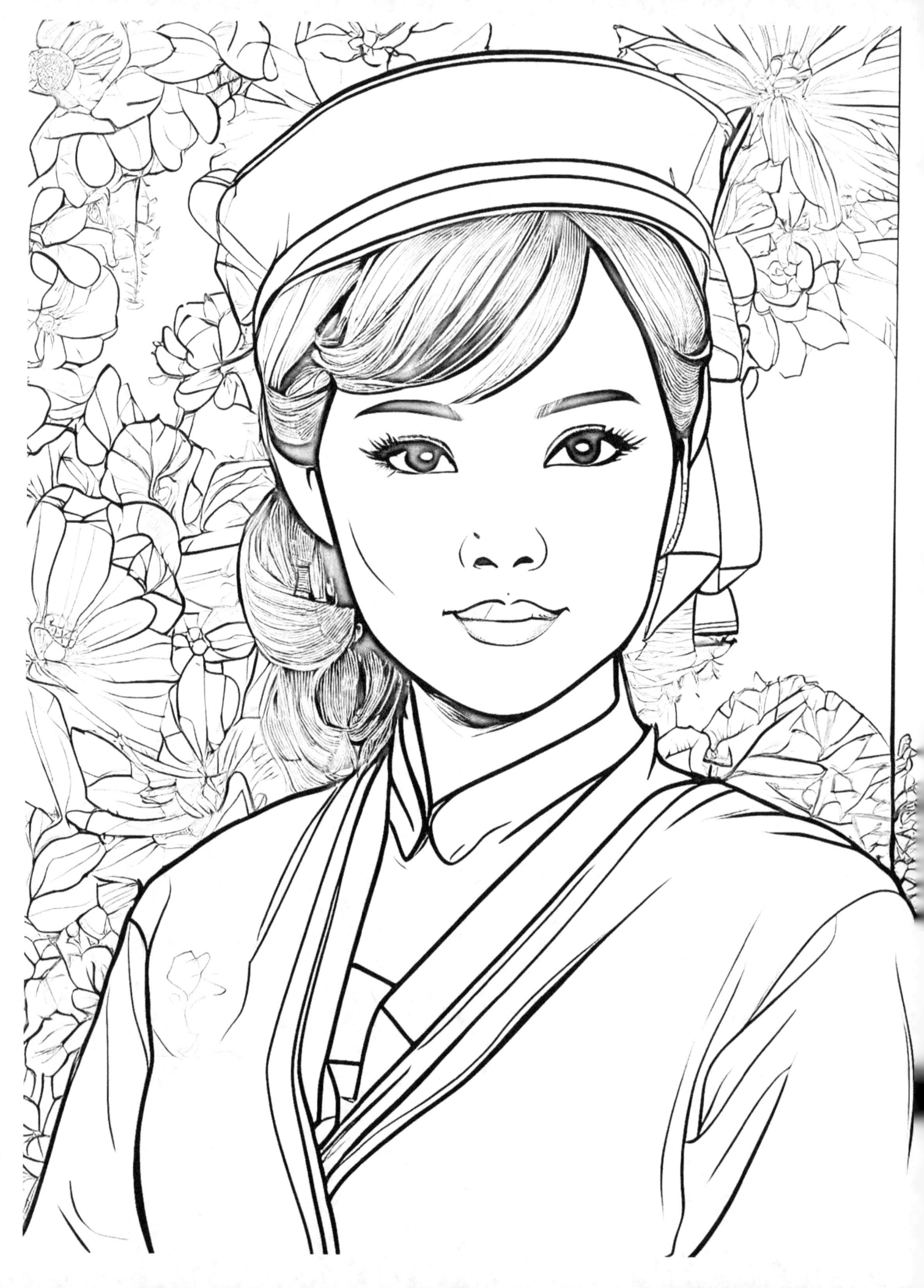

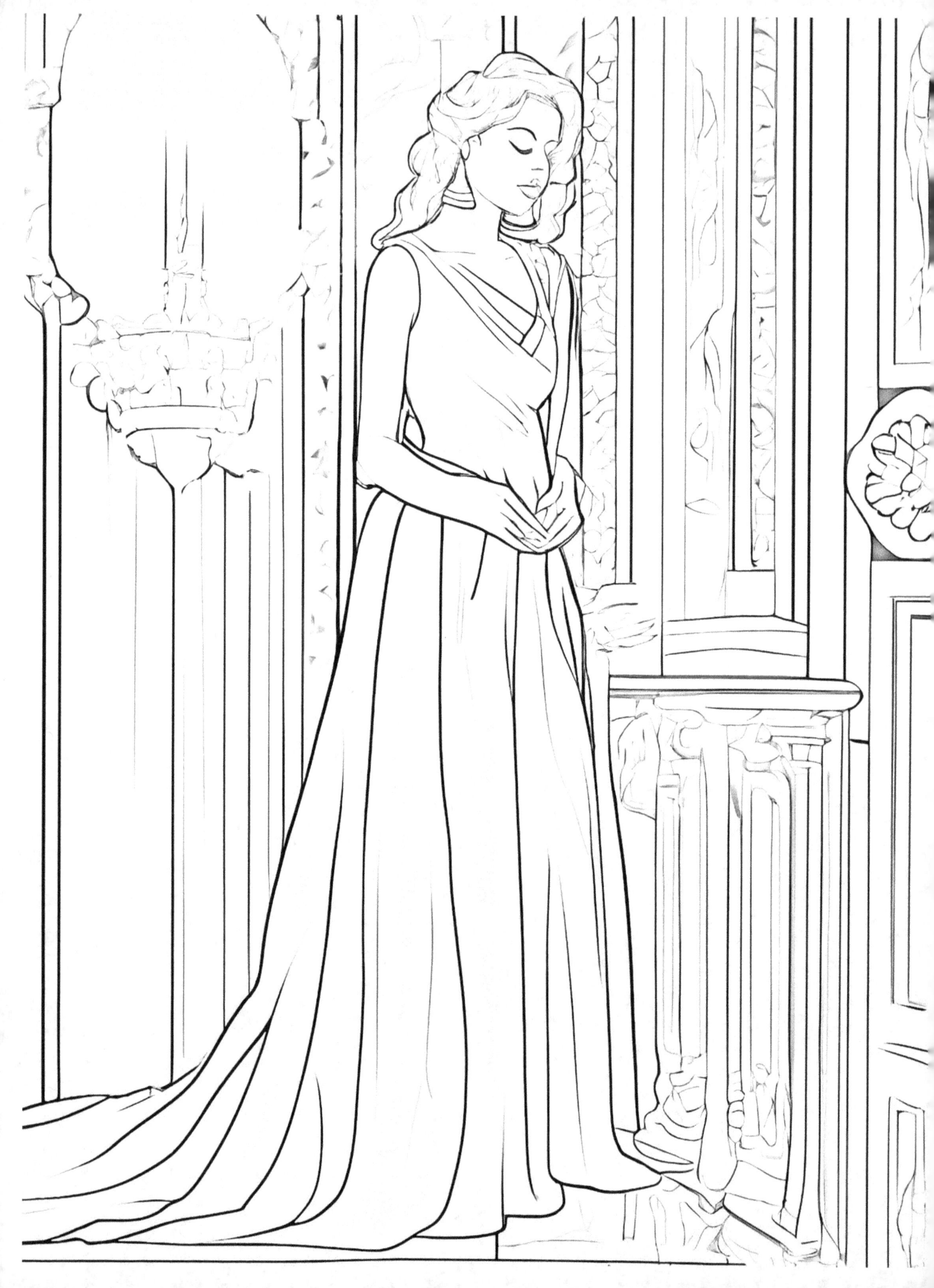

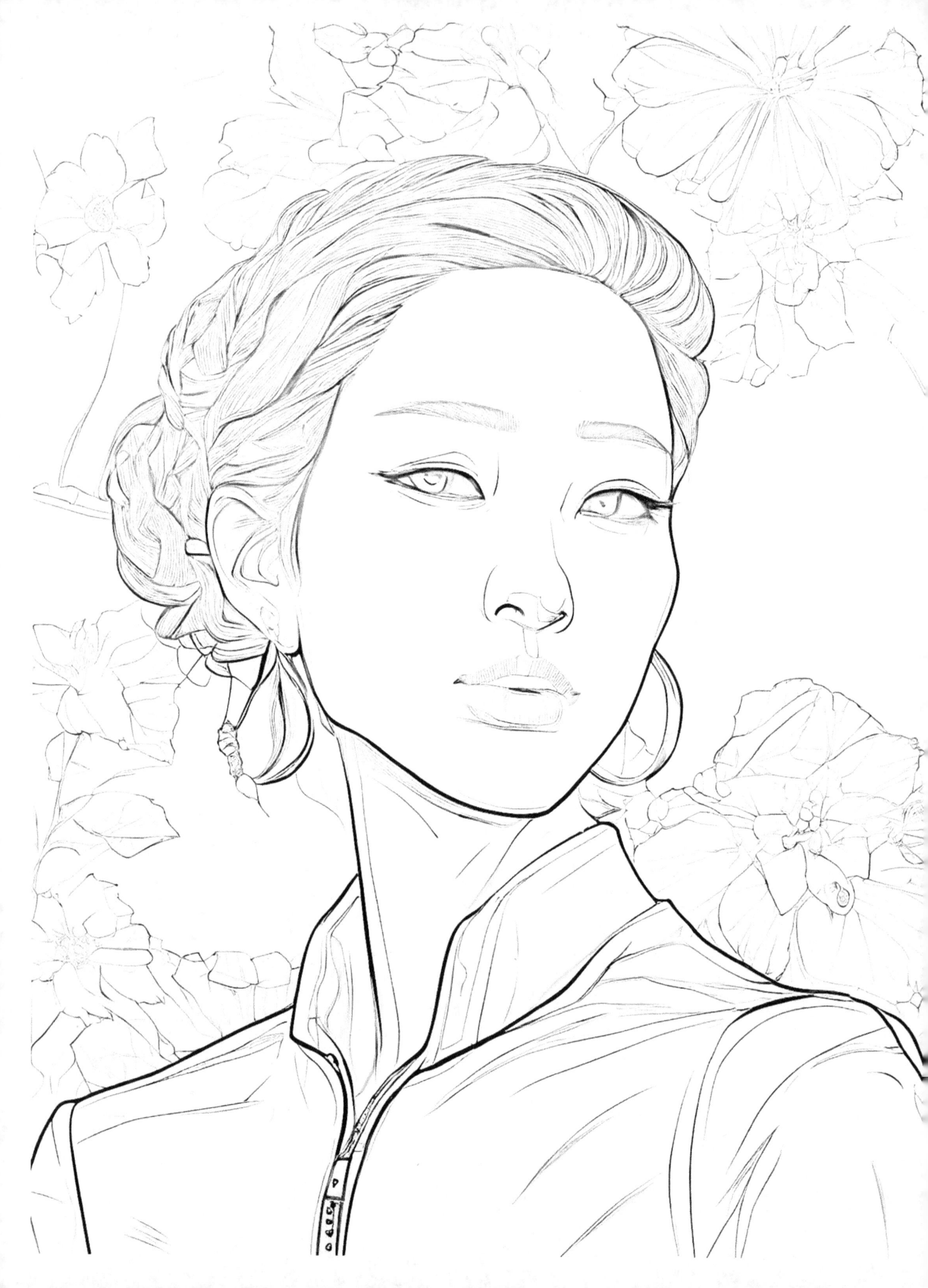

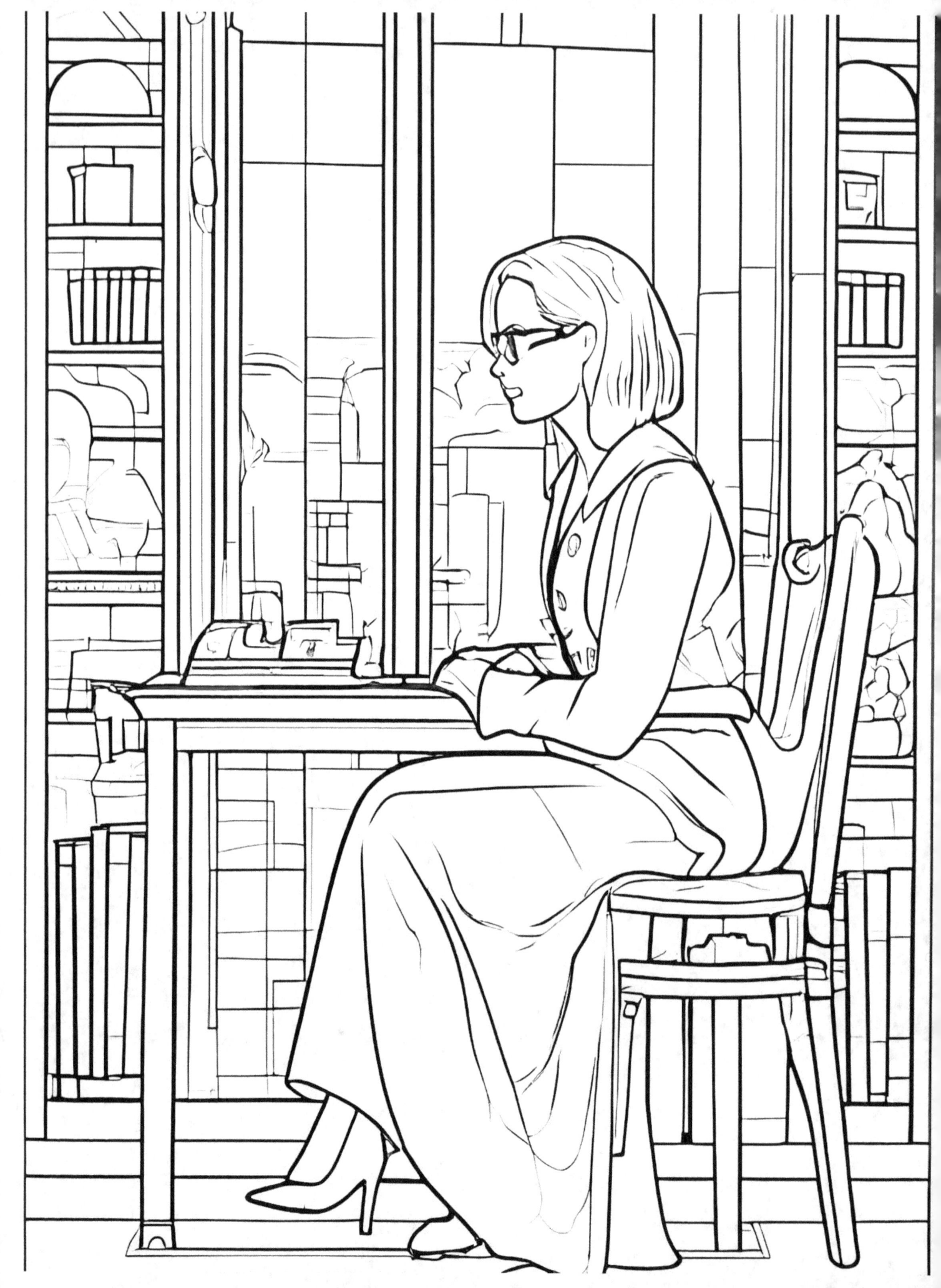

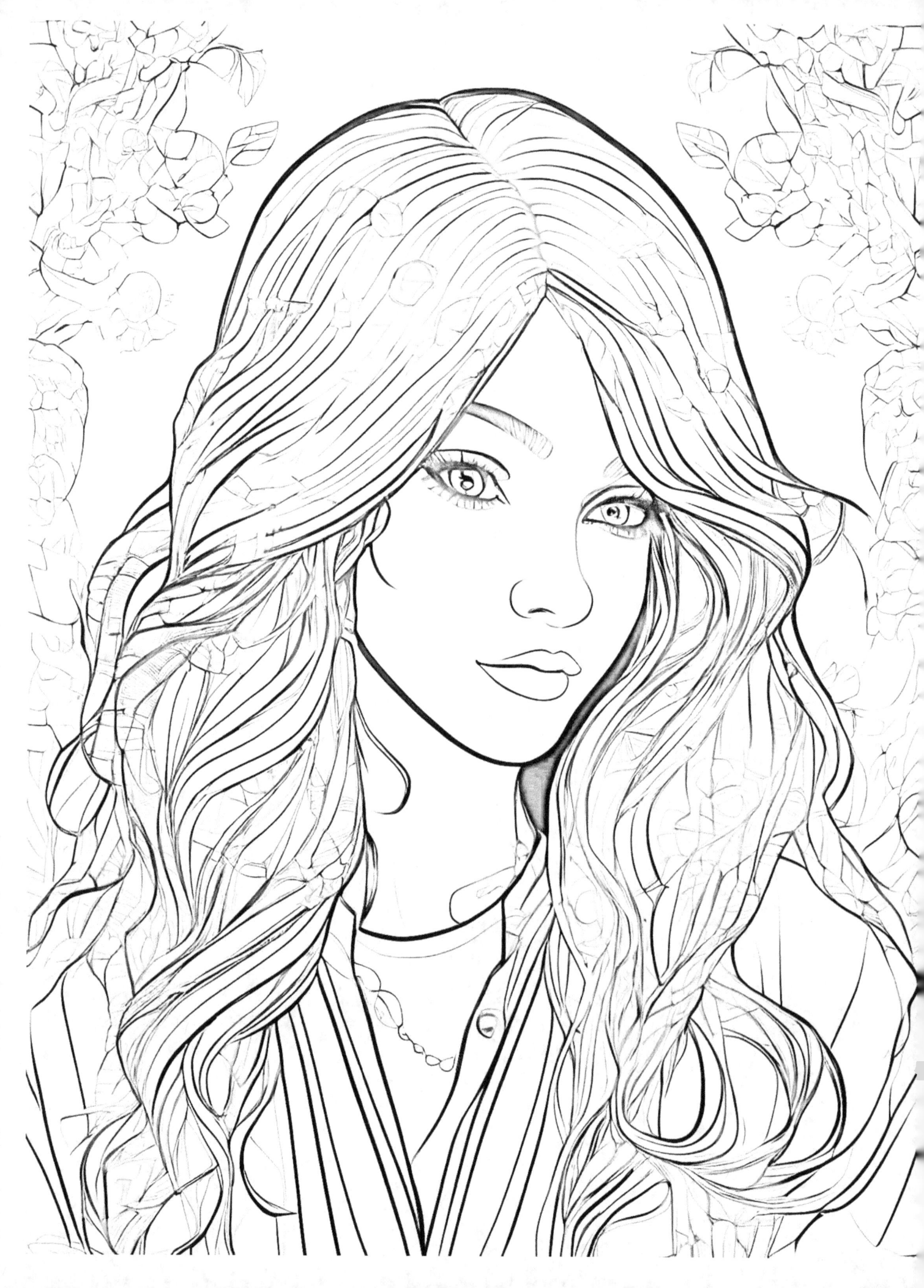

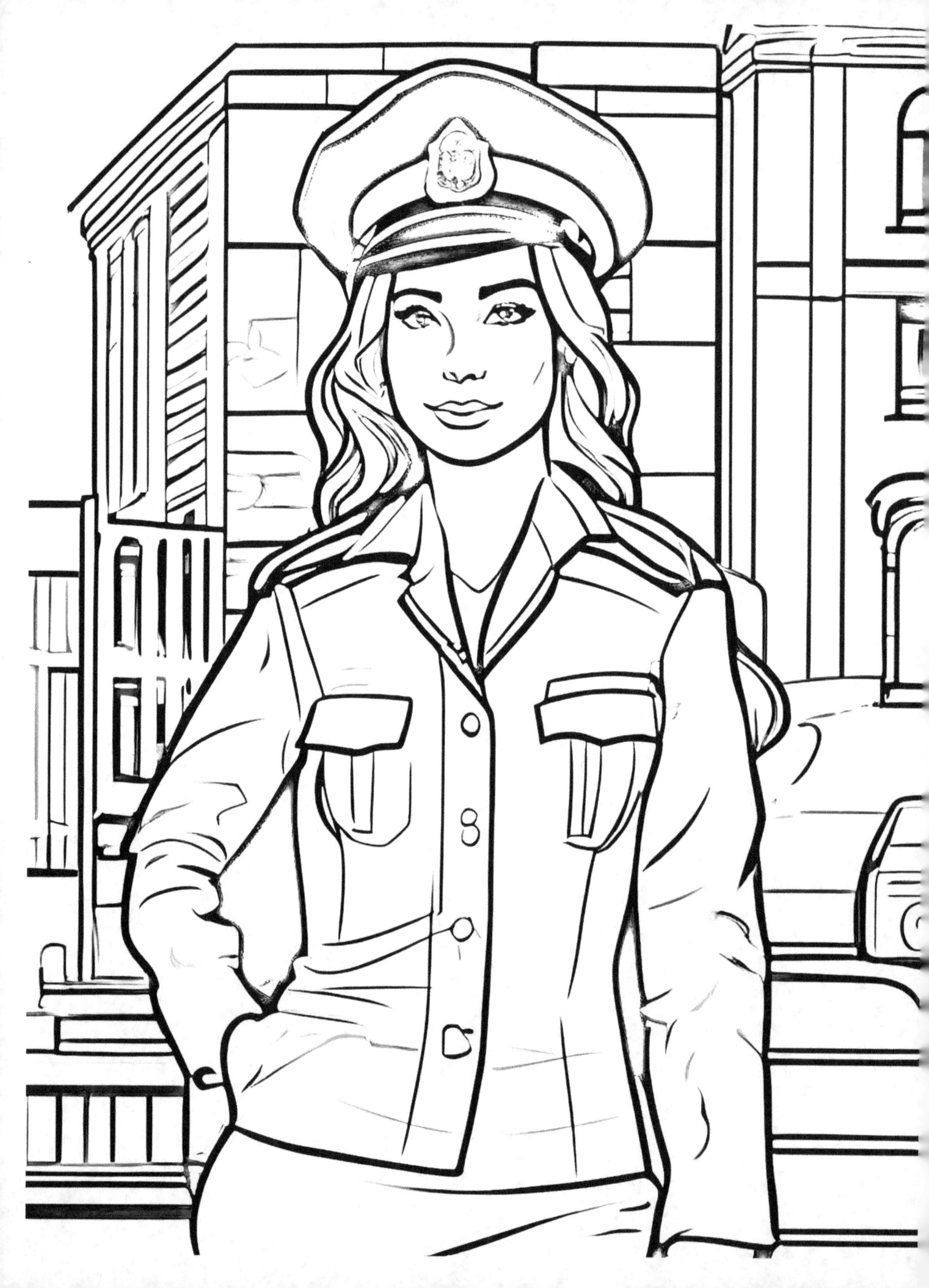

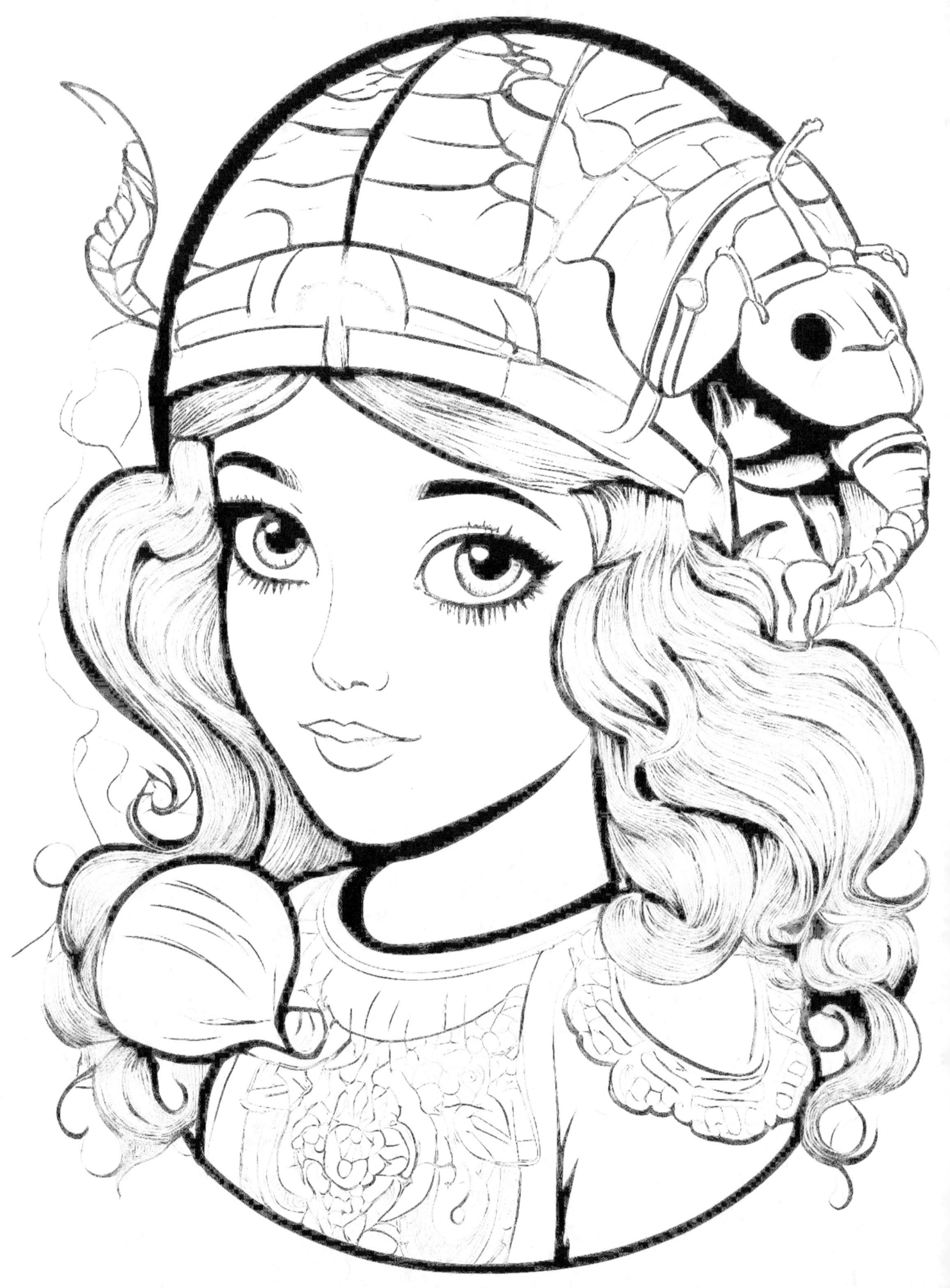

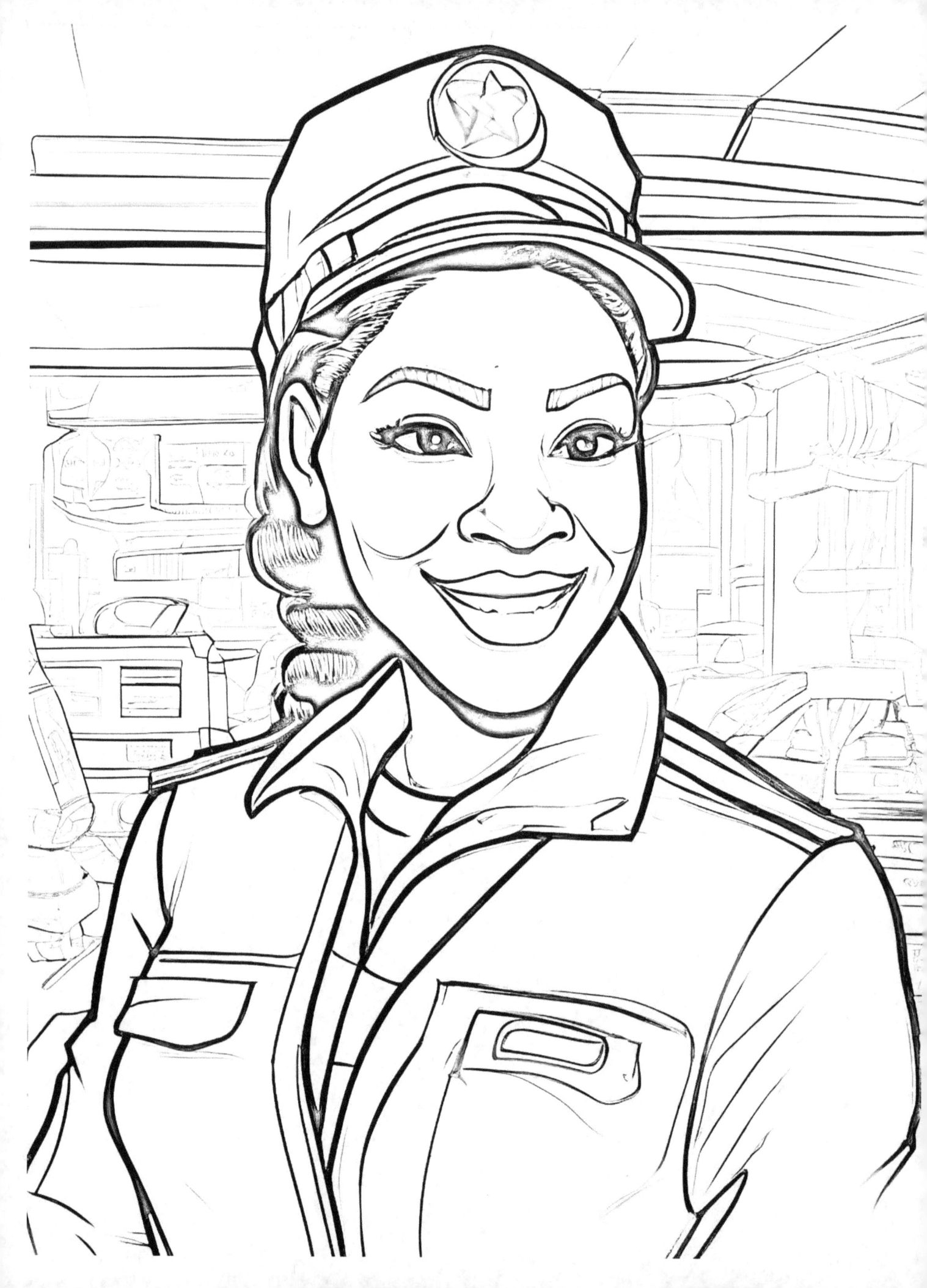

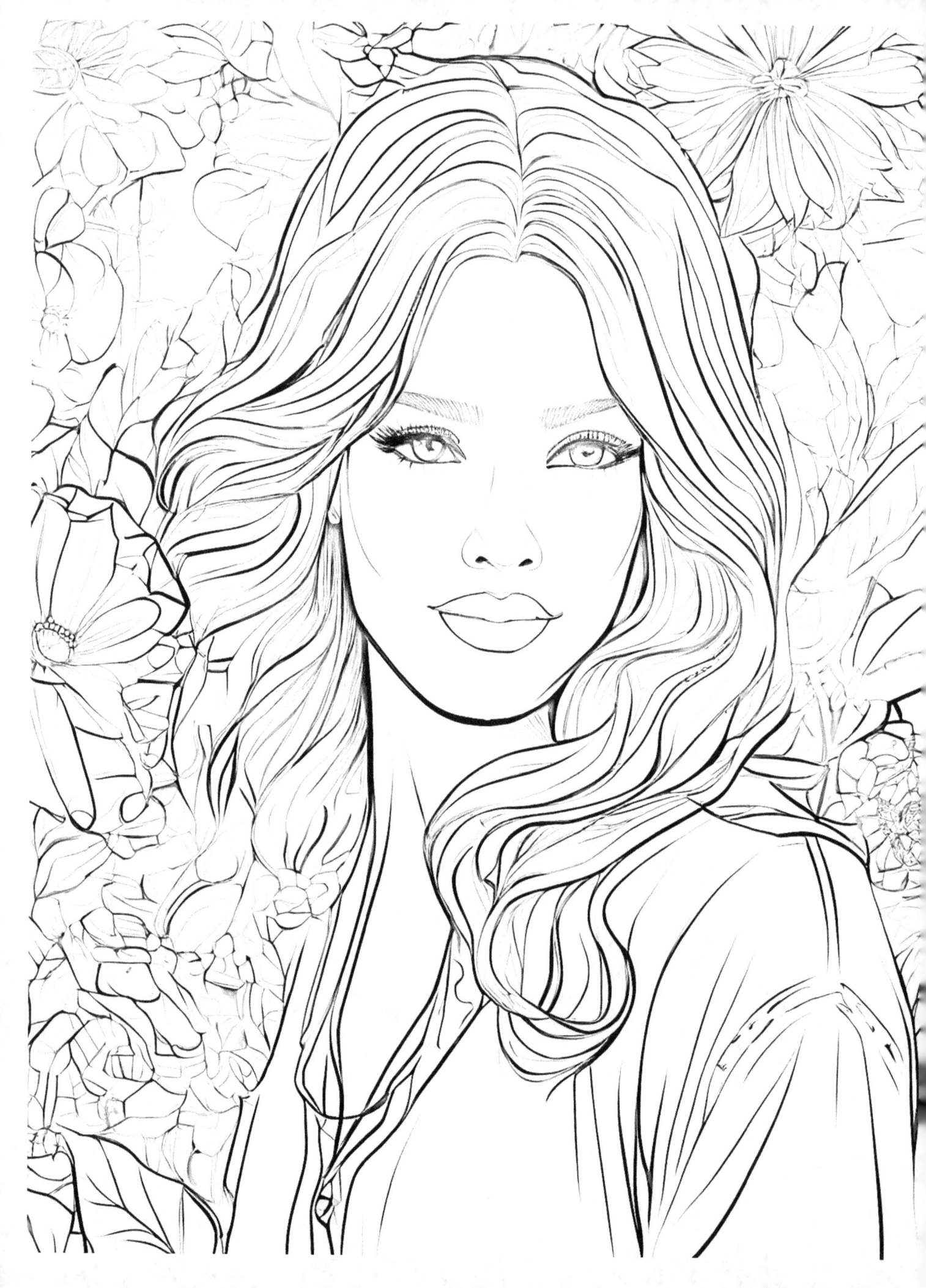

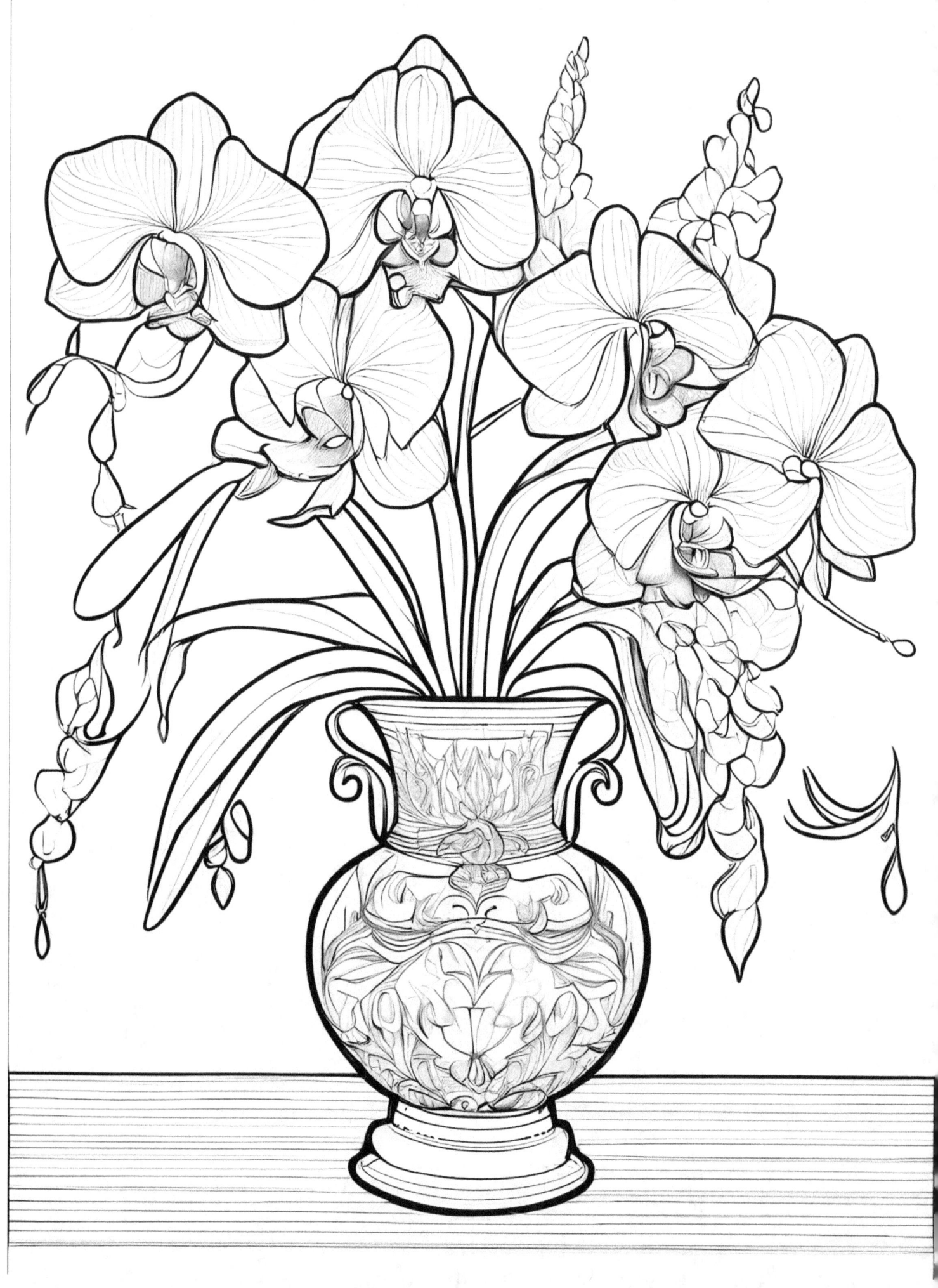

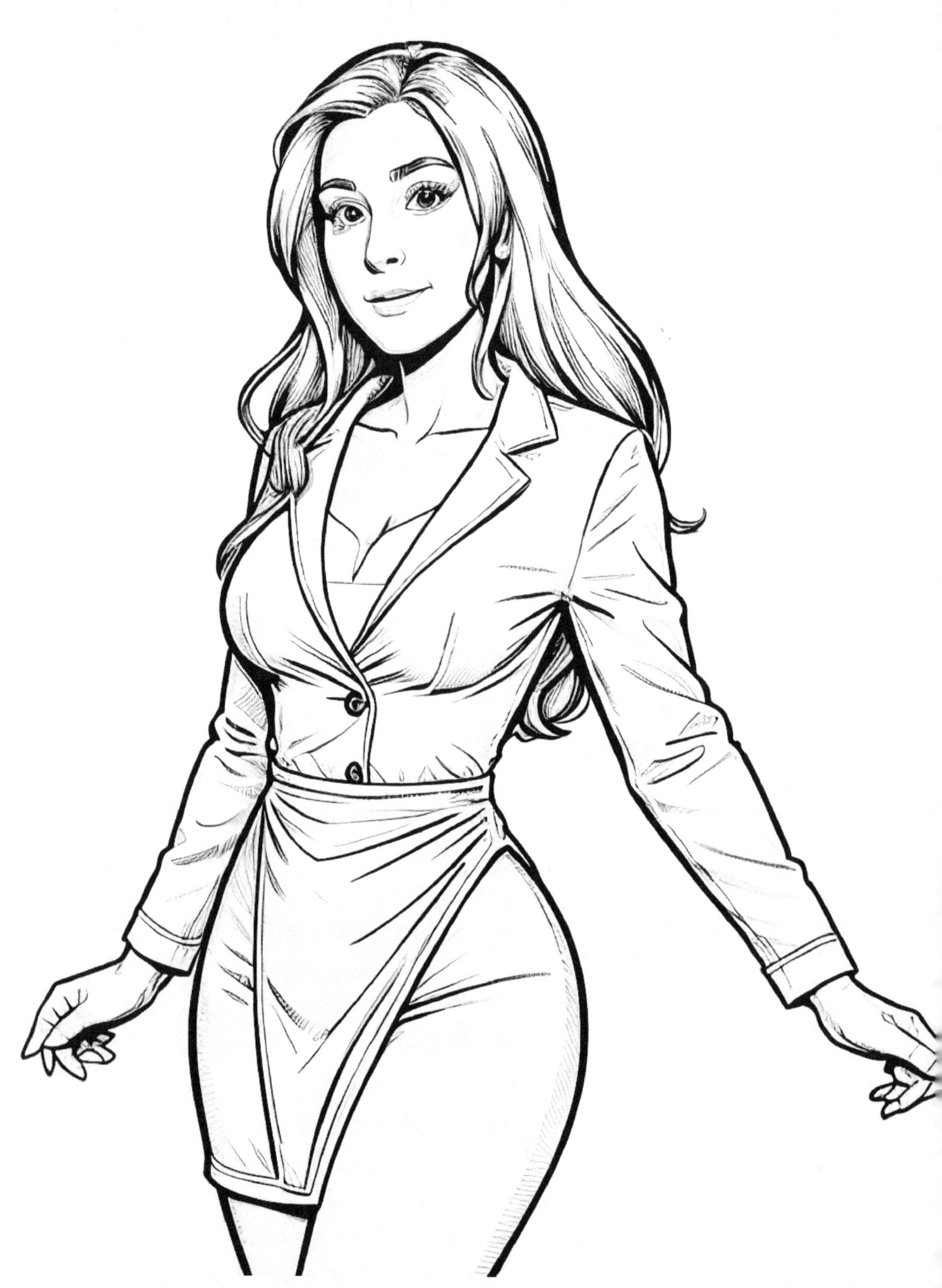

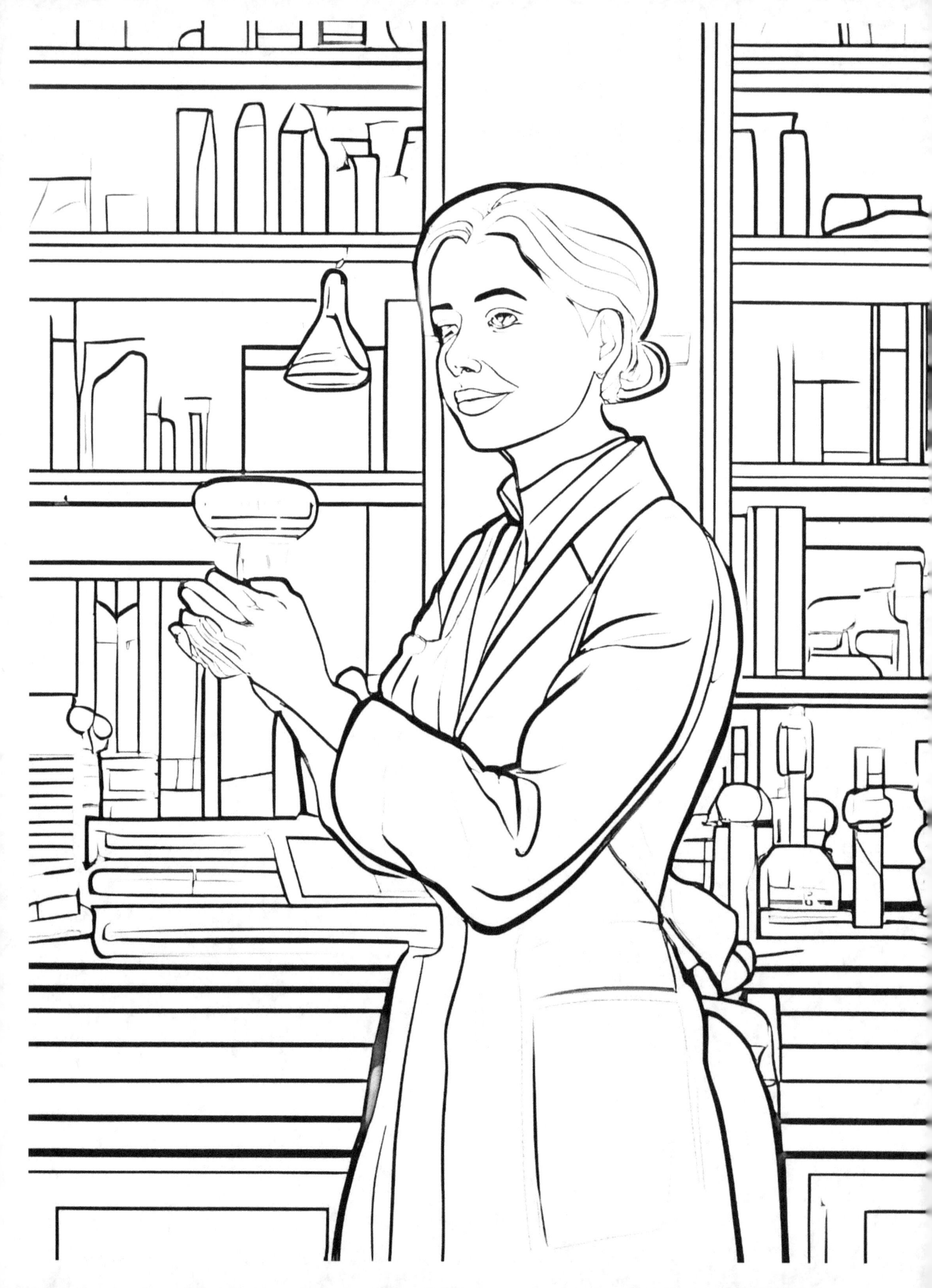

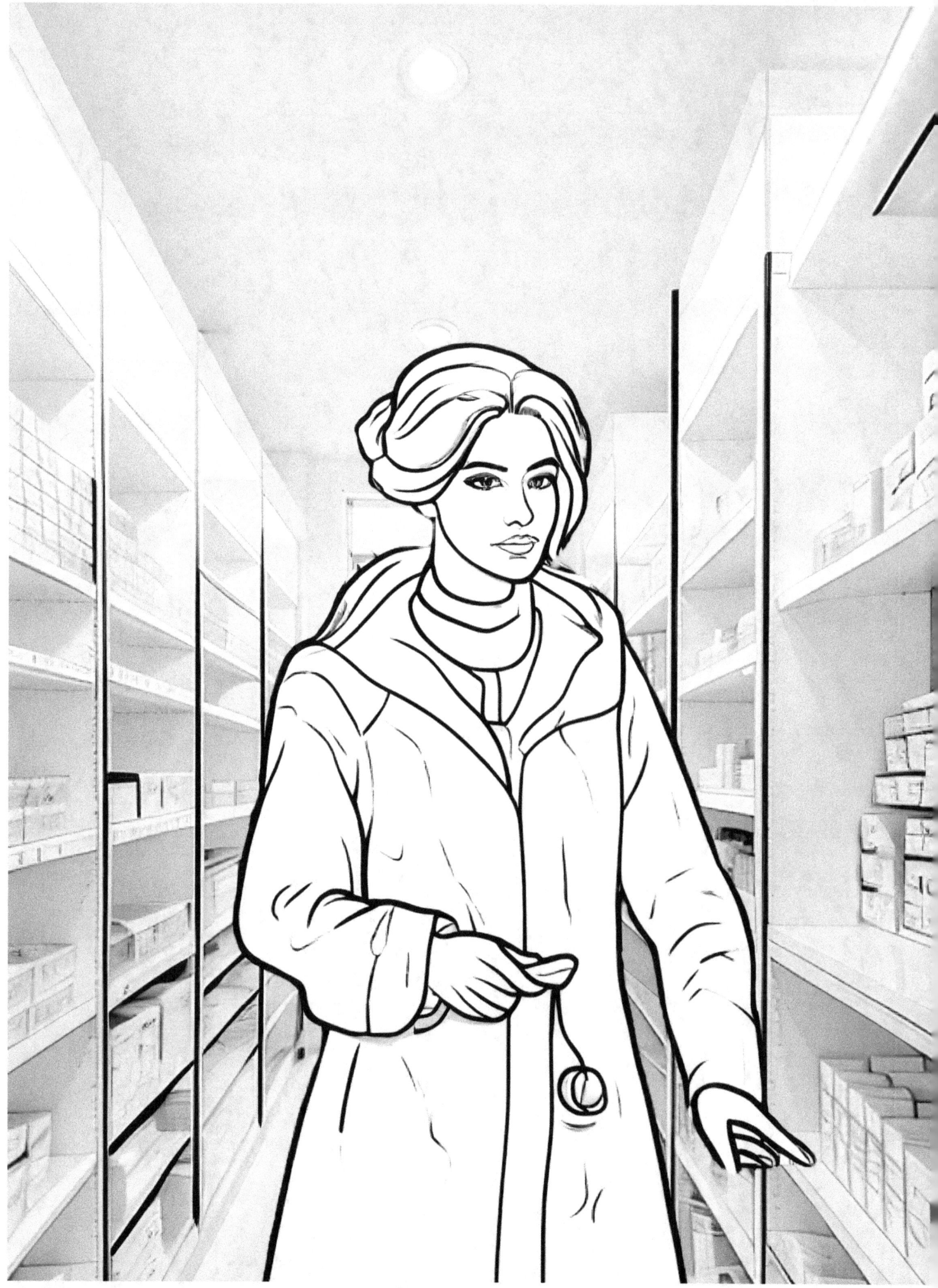

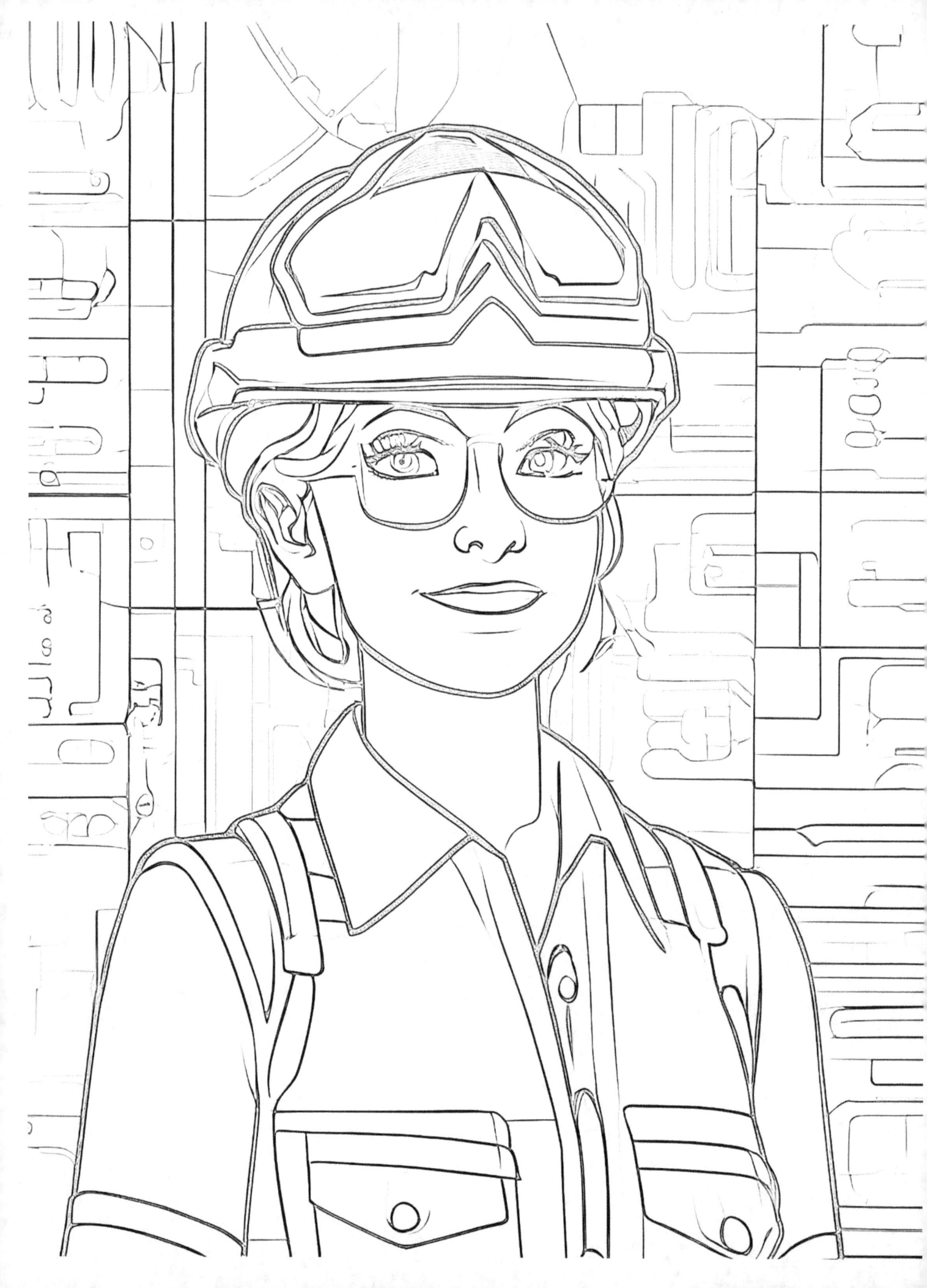

www.ingramcontent.com/pod-product-compliance
Lightning Source LLC
Chambersburg PA
CBHW081000290526
45795CB00009B/3015